LEAD LEADERS

—— TRAINING GUIDE ——

Developing the
Character and Competency
to Lead Leaders

Mac Lake

MOVEMENTS
PUBLISHING

First published in 2019 by 100 Movements Publishing
www.100mpublishing.com

ISBN 978-1-7333727-0-1

To Andy

Acknowledgments

I've dreamed of writing this type of training book for years. So much training material either focuses solely on leadership competencies or on the character of the leader. So I wanted to provide something that worked together to provide both. Over the years I have watched leaders grow in their leadership but then be "taken out" because of a flaw in their character. Conversely, I have seen leaders who are godly men or women but are unable to mobilize people because of a lack of leadership competencies. As we develop leaders, we must help them grow in both character and competency.

One of my "life verses" is Psalm 78:72: "David shepherded them with integrity of heart; with skillful hands, he led them." David was a great leader because he had both leadership skill and leadership spirit. When a leader has both, he or she is able to unite people together and mobilize them to make a kingdom impact.

I am thankful for the encouragement and support of so many on this journey. I want to thank: Will Mancini for believing in me and helping me identify my unique contribution in the kingdom; Alan Hirsch for his kindness and continual gentle encouragement for me to have the courage to publish what I write; Anna Robinson, the amazing editor and project manager, who continued pushing me to make this better and kept me focused and moving forward; and all the churches that have been through the Leadership Pipeline training that continually urged me to write these training modules.

Contents

Dear Friend   9

What Should I Know Before I Start?   11

Notes for the Trainer   19

Overview of Modules   23

Module 1: Practicing Spiritual Leadership   27

Module 2: Practicing Values-Based Leadership   55

Module 3: Bringing Out the Best in Your Leaders   75

Module 4: Leading Huddles   101

Module 5: Recruiting New Leaders   125

Module 6: Navigating Conflict   147

Module 7: Review Your Progress   173

Huddle Samples   195

Trainer Guide   203

Dear Friend,

Welcome to *Leading Leaders: Developing the Character and Competency to Lead Leaders*. This is your opportunity to advance in your development so that you learn both the character and competency necessary to lead leaders more effectively.

The *Discipling Leaders Series* outlines a strategy for developing a pipeline from which churches can draw and develop new leaders from within and move them along an intentional developmental pathway of growth on a personal and professional level. Each level of the Leadership Pipeline expands a leader's scope of responsibility in conjunction with their spiritual growth.

Leading The Church

Leading Departments

Leading Leaders

Leading Others

Leading Self

The Leadership Pipeline in a church begins with leading self. This is where the majority of people will be in the average congregation.

Most churches utilize small groups, Sunday School, or one-on-one mentoring to disciple those who are learning to lead themselves. While this is a critical step in every believer's journey, the scope of this series is not to cover the aspect of leading self. In my experience, many churches struggle with the discipleship of leaders. Therefore this series will focus on the discipleship of leaders at the various levels of the pipeline in the church.

Leading Leaders is the second book in the *Discipling Leaders Series*. Each level has specific skill sets and character traits that must be mastered in order to have a full range of expertise before moving to another leadership level:

Leading Others
Leading Leaders
Leading Departments
Leading the Church

I've discovered that most organizations structure for function, but they never think about structuring for development. The Leadership Pipeline framework gives a strategy for developing leaders from within your church, rather than having to hire from the outside. We have often defaulted to the easy route of "buying" leaders from the outside, rather than building leaders from within. The *Discipling Leaders Series* helps equip those who have the call, the character, and the competencies to move to new levels of leadership in your church.

I hope you enjoy this journey,

Mac Lake

What Should I Know Before I Start?

What Makes This Training Guide Unique?

1. An Apprenticeship Approach

This training requires the assistance and accountability of a trainer, normally someone your church leadership designates. Although you will work though the content of each module on your own, you will discuss your responses and reflections with a trainer. The trainer functions as both a mentor and a model of the core character traits and competencies needed to develop the next level of leadership. You will learn and grow under their leadership, as they observe your strengths and speak into your specific growth areas. In each module, you will be required to put into practice the principles you're learning. The trainer will give you opportunities to practice in the context of their leadership role and ministry by sharing some responsibilities and leadership tasks with you—it is intended to be an apprenticeship approach to your development. In fact, this guide can be worked through with up to two others meeting with you and your trainer as a small learning cohort. Having other learners beside you in the process will significantly increase your learning, as together you discuss your insights and discoveries along the way. This team approach is a return to the ancient form of mentoring that Jesus used with his disciples.

2. A Focus on Character and Competency

In each module, the focus is on two elements of leadership: deepening your *Character* and developing your *Competency*. The principle behind this structure is to develop the *skills* of a leader in sync with the *soul* of a true leader. When you operate both in tandem, your character can accommodate the acquisition of skills and can execute them in a godly manner that honors the principles taught in God's Word.

What Is the Philosophy of This Training?

This training is designed to produce transformation in your skills, not just help you absorb information. Lots of time and thought went into the structure of this material. I believe transformation happens in a triad of development with three overlapping factors:

1. Knowledge

In order to develop specific competencies, you need to learn key information about how to actually do the associated skills.

For example, if I wanted to improve my golf swing, I could buy a golf magazine featuring an article on five steps to the perfect swing. After reading and digesting the information, does it improve my swing? Not really. It does, however, give me some good information on the skills of a good swing.

2. Experience

If you want to experience transformation in your leadership character or competencies, you must put that competency into practice. That's where learning really begins to accelerate. It's the experience that allows you to see where you're strong and where you need to grow. It's practice that produces failure and frustration, and that's a good thing because it raises questions, which then leads to greater learning. Practice can also lead to success, which produces greater levels of learning and confidence in that particular leadership skill.

Let's go back to my golf example. I'm trying to improve my golf swing. I read the article on the five steps to the perfect golf swing. That gives me the knowledge. But then I need experience. So, I grab a nine iron, go to my backyard, and swing a thousand times. Now, does that improve my swing? Not necessarily. If I'm doing things the right way, I may improve. But it may make things worse if I'm swinging incorrectly. When I make the same mistake repeatedly, I am reinforcing a bad habit.

3. Coaching

In order to develop your leadership competencies, you also need someone to observe you in action, give you feedback and discuss what you are learning in the process. The coaching portion is where learning is solidified. The trainer/coach can give further assignments, which can lead to further practice, which will lead to further growth.

Once again, let's go back to improving my golf swing. So far I have read the article and practiced my swing in my backyard. Now I'm going to invite my friend who's a golf pro to come and observe my swing and give me feedback. As he's watching, he says, "Whoa, whoa, wait a minute, Mac. Keep your head down. Hold on, keep your left arm straight. Bend those knees." As he gives me this feedback, my swing begins to improve, new habits are developed, and eventually I produce a nice swing that enables me to lower my score by seven strokes. Success!

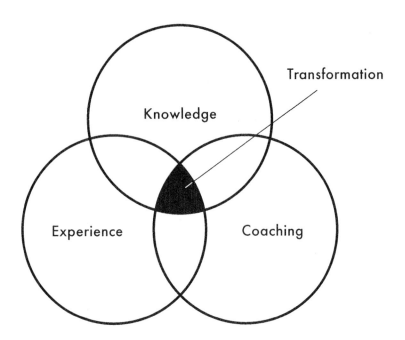

The focus is on *transformation*, not just the exchange of information. When you practice all three of these elements on a consistent basis, then you see transformation really start to happen.

How Do I Get the Most out of These Modules?

You may have previously participated in leadership training and at the time thought it was really great. Yet, a few days later, you're unsure how to apply what you've learned or simply can't remember it. To ensure this is not your experience here, follow these tips:

- Work through the content for the module on your own, making sure you have enough time and headspace to fully engage with the questions. Write your answers and thoughts in the space that is provided throughout the modules.
- Don't just read the "Put it into Practice" section. Take it seriously and recognize it is the *practice* of this skill that will help

you grow in that area. Take every opportunity to practice what you are learning, whether in your home, work, or church context. This practice will sharpen your skill and build your leadership confidence.

- Every other week, meet with your trainer and up to two other trainees to discuss your reflections. Come to each session ready to share what you learned from the reading and from putting this skill into practice. Your trainer will be someone who is experienced at leading leaders and can give you feedback, insights, and ideas that will better equip you to do the same.
- Shadow your trainer as he or she is leading in their ministry area. Following them around, attending a huddle they are leading, or watching them engage one-on-one with one of their leaders can be a valuable learning experience as they model healthy leadership to you.

How Long Will the Training Take?

One of the first questions people ask is: How long will it take me to finish this training? The goal is not to "finish" or "get through" the training. The goal is shaping your character and competencies as a leader of leaders. Some people will learn and adapt quickly. Others will require more time and practice. Some will come into this training with previous leadership experience, while others may be totally new at leading leaders. Ideally, you can take up to two weeks to complete each module. Meet with your trainer every other week. But don't rush. And don't cram. Pace yourself as a learner to digest the material and put it into practice.

Because *Discipling Leaders* is a discipleship-based, rather than a traditional classroom-based, training, there is a flexible timeline for you to complete each module. In other words, this mentoring/discipleship-based approach means you may or may not cover one module in one meeting. You and your trainer may choose to spend several meetings on one topic to ensure you're developing the character and competency for that module. The objective is to demonstrate growth, not just absorb the information.

How Is Each Module Organized?

The modules are very interactive and will require you to write down your answers and reflections. Each module includes various sections that will help you learn more rapidly, including:

■ Learning Objectives

Focus points to learn as a result of this study. Though you may gain additional learning from the modules, the objectives are designed to guide you to these particular outcomes.

■ Pre-Assessment

Assess your current character and competency before you begin a module.

■ Questions

Process the information and spark transformative discussion.

■ Deepen Your Character

A character trait study of Scripture that undergirds each competency.

■ Develop Your Competency

Content and follow-up questions to develop a particular competency.

■ Put It into Practice

Assignments to complete and/or review with your trainer.

■ Reflect on Your Learning

Questions to help you reflect on your key learning for the module.

Now that you understand the uniqueness of this training and have a big picture overview, let's dive in and get started.

Notes for the Trainer

As a trainer, you are both a *model* and a *mentor*.

As a **model**, you allow those you are training to watch you demonstrate both the character and competency each module refers to. You are the best curriculum others can read.

As a **mentor**, you observe and give trainees feedback as they put what they're learning into practice. Approach your time together with the spirit of a fellow learner, rather than the spirit of a teacher. The mentoring component is best accomplished by training two to three people at one time, rather than going through it one-on-one. With this dynamic, you'll have better discussions and the participants will learn from one another as well.

Training can occur in any place, at any time, at any pace. Establish a rhythm that works for you, based on those you're training. Bi-monthly meetings will give those you are training time to complete a module and put it into practice. However, remember the purpose is *transformation* resulting from growth in the character and competency of those you are training, so do not rush modules. Feel free to meet two or even three times for one module if you feel that's necessary. One of the beauties of this approach to training is you can have a flexible timeline.

Follow the flow of questions in the Trainer Guide. There is a Trainer Guide at the back of the book that puts all the questions together or you can choose to simply follow the questions as they are laid out in the modules. Don't skip around—talk through the questions/answers and the assessments in the order they appear in each module. Drive the participants to a next step of action and/or insight. Feel free to ask follow-up questions to increase learning. Follow a five-part agenda for each session:

 ## 1. Connect (5–10 minutes)

Spend the first few minutes allowing the group to connect relationally, catch up on what's been going on in their week. Avoid just rushing into the content. Remember you want this to be a relational approach to development, which means allowing people time to get to know each other well.

 ## 2. Celebrate (5 minutes)

Ask, "What is something we've seen God do since the last time we met that we can celebrate?" You don't have to spend a lot of time on this, but take a few minutes and enjoy the work God is doing in their lives or in their ministries. This celebration time can reveal some important things in the lives of these leaders and can deepen their faith as they watch how God is working in each other's lives.

 ## 3. Coach (30–45 minutes)

Walk through all the questions and assessments. The trainee should have worked through all the content of the module before you meet with them, so you are asking them to discuss issues they have already considered and reflected on personally. The material provided is more than enough for

NOTES FOR THE TRAINER | 21

a forty-five-minute discussion. Make sure you are prepared to discuss what is most relevant for your particular learners. As already mentioned, you may choose to spend more than one meeting to cover one module.

4. Communicate (1–2 minutes)

Ask, "What important upcoming events do we all need to be aware of?" You won't need to spend much more than one minute on this. But it is important to communicate any key events coming up at the church as well as the details for your next training session.

5. Care (10–15 minutes)

Make sure you save time to ask, "How can we pray for each other?" Spend a few minutes praying with and for each other.

Each session should be around fifty to seventy-five minutes.

Overview of Modules

In *Leading Leaders,* you will develop the following competencies and deepen your character by completing these modules:

Module 1: Practicing Spiritual Leadership

Character: *Courage*
Leaders take bold steps of faith in the face of obstacles and opposition.

Competency: *Spiritual Leadership*
Develop the heart and practices of a spiritual leader so you can leave a legacy for others to emulate.

Module 2: Practicing Values-Based Leadership

Character: *Integrity*
Leaders are honest and demonstrate consistent character.

Competency: *Values-Based Leadership*
Embody your values and lead in a way to create practices and patterns that reflect those values and move the team toward the common goal and vision.

Module 3: Bringing out the Best in Your Leaders

Character: *Encouragement*
Leaders encourage others in such a way that it shapes their soul.

Competency: *Bring out the Best in Others*
Learn how to bring out the best in others through encouraging and challenging them toward maximizing their strengths.

Module 4: Leading Huddles

Character: *Humility*
Leaders consider the needs of others above their own.

Competency: *Leading Huddles*
Lead a huddle in a way that unites, develops, and challenges members to more effectively lead their team/group.

Module 5: Recruiting New Leaders

Character: *Passion*
Leaders are filled with a fervent drive toward the cause God has given them.

Competency: *Recruiting Leaders*
Expand your team by following a deliberate recruitment process.

Module 6: Navigating Conflict

Character: *Patience*

Leaders must be gentle when navigating conflict and bear with others' shortcomings with the higher goal of developing their spiritual maturity.

Competency: *Navigating Conflict*

Manage conflict in a way that honors God and those involved.

Module 7: Review Your Progress

Self-evaluate to discover your strengths and your areas for growth.

1

Practicing Spiritual Leadership

Introduction

As a leader of leaders you will be helping other leaders grow in their leadership role. Often when we think about leadership development, we think of developing a leader's skills. But when we only focus on developing a leader's competency, and neglect the development of their character, we may be setting them up for short-term success, rather than long-term sustainability and spiritual impact. You see, it's leadership character, and an abiding faith in Christ, that enables a leader to endure the rigors of leadership and leave a great leadership legacy. In this module we will focus on deepening your courage and developing your competency of spiritual leadership.

Deepen Your Character: Courage
Leaders take bold steps of faith in the face of obstacles and opposition.

Develop Your Competency: *Spiritual Leadership*
Develop the heart and practices of a spiritual leader so you can leave a legacy for others to emulate.

Objectives

1. Using Paul's example of courageous leadership, identify a specific way you can grow in your leadership courage.

2. Describe specific insights you've gained from observing other spiritual leaders in action.

3. Identify reasons leaders may not respond enthusiastically to your leadership.

4. Articulate how you would teach a young leader to shape the character of the people on his or her team.

5. Grow in spiritual leadership conversations with a leader using the 5-P Agenda taught in this module.

Deepen Your Character: Courage

Courage is the engine that fuels the heart and soul of spiritual leaders. It allows leaders to live with integrity, to stand up for what is important, and to speak out when necessary. But there are times when all leaders face situations where fear raises its head and they are tempted to compromise, people please, or doubt God's faithfulness. Part of God's plan for your character is to deepen your faith in him, which means there will be times you have to demonstrate great faith and act courageously even in the face of fear.

Paul models such courageous leadership in Acts 20. This passage recounts Paul's farewell to the leaders at the church of Ephesus before heading to Jerusalem in time for the day of Pentecost. He loved these men and knew they would face opposition and criticism in the days ahead. And so, in his farewell speech to these leaders he reminds them of the example he set for them: "You know how I lived the whole time I was with you." Throughout this speech, many of the qualities of a courageous spiritual leader are demonstrated.

Scripture

As you read the following Scripture, meditate on what the author wishes to communicate, and answer the questions below. Allow the Holy Spirit to speak to you and challenge you as a leader about how you can develop your character in this area of courage.

Acts 20:17–27

From Miletus, Paul sent to Ephesus for the elders of the church. When they arrived, he said to them: "You know how I lived the whole time I was with you, from the first day I came into the province of Asia. I served the Lord with great humility and with tears and in the midst of severe testing by the plots of my Jewish opponents. You know that I have not hesitated to preach anything that would be helpful to you but have taught you publicly and from house to house. I have declared to both Jews and Greeks that they must turn to God in repentance and have faith in our Lord Jesus.

"And now, compelled by the Spirit, I am going to Jerusalem, not knowing what will happen to me there. I only know that in every city the Holy Spirit warns me that prison and hardships are facing me. However, I consider my life worth nothing to me; my only aim is to finish the race and complete the task the Lord Jesus has given me—the task of testifying to the good news of God's grace.

"Now I know that none of you among whom I have gone about preaching the kingdom will ever see me again. Therefore, I declare to you today that I am innocent of the blood of any of you. For I have not hesitated to proclaim to you the whole will of God."

Think of a time you saw courageous leadership in action. How did that courageous act impact you personally?

This passage is laced with evidence that Paul was a courageous leader. List the words or phrases in this passage where you see examples of his leadership courage:

To assess the measure of your character, let's look at how well you consistently demonstrate courage as a spiritual leader. To begin, make a list of at least three traits of a courageous leader that you see demonstrated in this passage. Write them on the next page and mark each trait red, yellow or green.

Red = I am not demonstrating this area.

Yellow = I could be more intentional in this area.

Green = I am demonstrating this consistently.

1.

2.

3.

Write down one insight this exercise reveals about your character.

Write down one action step you need to take to grow in courage.

Having examined the character trait of courage, we can now begin to work through the core competency for this module: **Develop the heart and practices of a spiritual leader so you can leave a legacy for others to emulate**.

As you read through this section, note how the character trait of courage can undergird a leader's competency of spiritual leadership.

Develop Your Competency: *Spiritual Leadership*
Pre-Assessment

Before proceeding, complete the assessment below. In the final module of this training guide, you will retake it as a post-assessment to measure your transformation and growth regarding this competency.

The following proficiencies demonstrate mastery of this module's competency.

Grade yourself on each of these proficiencies A, B, C, D or E. Giving yourself an A+ indicates you are a model for others to follow. An E indicates no mastery.

Proficiency	Pre-Assessment
I am constantly making efforts to grow spiritually.	
I regularly connect relationally with those I am leading.	
I consistently challenge those I am leading.	
I practice active listening.	
I prioritize praying for my leaders.	

Reflection Questions

Who do you think is the most admired spiritual leader in America today?

Why?

Demonstrating Spiritual Leadership

When you step into leadership, you have a strong desire that God will use you to advance his mission and impact the lives of the people around you. But we've all witnessed leaders who have imploded because of bad personal decisions. Or leaders who neglect their walk with God and, over time, are leading in their own strength, dependent upon their own wisdom, and making decisions based on a personal agenda. This is why it's critical as a leader of leaders you develop the heart and practices of a spiritual leader so you can leave a legacy for others to emulate. As you model Christlike leadership, the leaders around you will learn Christlike leadership.

Late into his public ministry, Jesus gave his disciples an instruction that would be crucial to the impact of their leadership. He said:

> "I am the true vine, and my Father is the gardener. He cuts off every branch in me that bears no fruit, while every branch that does bear fruit he prunes so that it will be even more fruitful. You are already clean because of the word I have spoken to you. *Remain in me*, as I also remain in you. No branch can bear fruit by itself; it must remain in the vine. Neither can you bear fruit unless you remain in me.
>
> "I am the vine; you are the branches. If you remain in me and I in you, you will bear much fruit; apart from me you can do nothing."
>
> John 15:1–5 (my italics)

As we learn to abide in Christ, we will hear his voice, know the promptings of the Spirit, and as a result be able to accomplish the work he desires for us in our leadership role.

Early in my ministry, I was fortunate to work for a pastor who was a model spiritual leader. Pastor Bob Barrows was a humble leader and full of integrity. Every week he would meet with me, ask me questions, get to know my heart and soul, and find ways to both encourage and challenge me. Under his leadership I was constantly growing in my character and leadership skills. To this day, I hold a deep affection and admiration for this spiritual leader who had such an impact on my life.

It's not just the degree of your competency that draws others to follow you. It's also the degree of your character.

Reflect on some of the people you have been led by.
What did you most admire about their character?

What leadership skill did they consistently demonstrate that made
them such a good leader?

What would you most like to emulate from the way they lead?

Two Keys to Becoming a Leader Worth Following

A young woman once confided after one of my workshops, "I'm so frustrated. I've been working with my team for a year, and I don't feel like they respect me or follow my leadership. I just don't know what to do."

This kind of complaint usually relates to two issues represented in what I've come to call my life verse. Psalm 78:72 says, "David shepherded them with integrity of heart; with skillful hands he led them." This one verse tells us two things that made David such a great leader: David had leadership *spirit* and leadership *skill*. In his spirit, he was a man who followed after God, and people loved that about David. He knew God and allowed him to shape his inner being. He was also a man who had leadership skill. God utilized his talents to do incredible things to build a great nation.

I've discovered that this combination of leadership spirit and skill is rare. Many leaders have one or the other, but earning the respect of your team requires both. Those with solely leadership spirit may have many loyal people following them. People love the leader's admirable character, but they only follow for so long until it becomes increasingly obvious that little is getting done. The mission is not being advanced.

Other leaders have great leadership skill and can implement an inspiring vision to the letter. But as much as they accomplish, if people do not feel valued, and sense they are just a cog in the machine, then they eventually bow out.

If you're struggling as a leader, feeling you aren't getting the respect of your team, I want to encourage you to evaluate.

Start with leadership *spirit*. Just take a moment and ask, "Am I demonstrating the fruit of the Spirit (love, joy, peace, etc.) to those that I'm leading? Am I praying for those on my team? Am I asking for God's empowering or am I trying to do it in my own strength?" If some of those qualities are missing, that may be why you're struggling to earn the respect of your team.

Next, evaluate your leadership *skill.* Maybe people love you, but they've stopped following you because they're not seeing progress toward the mission. Ask, "Am I empowering my team, or am I micromanaging them? Am I clarifying the expectations of the team or am I confusing them? Am I delegating to and developing them, or have I left them on their own? Am I providing a clear and compelling vision, or have I become complacent about the future?"

Make a list of leadership spirit characteristics and leadership skill requirements. Evaluate yourself against both lists and identify ways to make progress at your weakest points.

Leadership Spirit   Leadership Skill

What did this list reveal to you about areas you could grow in?

As you grow, be prepared to be amazed at how much your team's respect for you will increase!

Five Traits of a Spiritual Leader

You can spot spiritual leaders because of their common characteristics. As you read through the following traits, mentally associate each one with someone you know who consistently practices that quality.

1. Spiritual leaders are constantly growing

As leaders, there is a danger that we can become too enamored with our leadership role or too engrossed in ministry. We lose intimacy with God because we are so busy serving him.

In Romans 11:33, Paul describes the incredible and wonderous depths of God; we can spend a lifetime increasing our understanding of God's love and character. Spiritual leaders are continually pursuing greater knowledge of Christ and his work. First, we must constantly evaluate our personal desire for God. Ask yourself, "How 'thirsty' am I for God's Word and time alone with him?" Next, build in some disciplines to support your need to grow—expand your personal devotional time, do a Bible study with close friends, identify an accountability partner, or do a one-day spiritual retreat.

2. Spiritual leaders invite people into their lives

Time is one of the greatest gifts you can give to those you lead. Whenever we are providing leadership for others it involves a commitment to them. This means not only doing ministry together but also getting to know them on a personal level. Jesus interacted with many people before he chose twelve key men he would spend the majority of his time with. We know from Luke 6 that before Jesus selected these twelve, he spent the night in prayer. Luke describes the event this way: "At daybreak he called together all of his disciples and chose twelve of them to be apostles" (Luke 6:13 NLT). Isn't it interesting that he called "all of his disciples" together? How many were standing at the foot of the mountain that day? We don't know, but we do know that as he looked at the group gathered there, he only selected twelve of them to be on his core team as apostles.

Jesus wasn't choosing a group of strangers. No, he had known and interacted with these twelve for months by this point. I have to believe Jesus' choice reflected both a high confidence in, and a deep connection with, these men. By inviting the twelve into this special relationship, Jesus was committing to invest in them and share his life with them.

3. Spiritual leaders pray for those they are leading

Paul told Timothy in 2 Timothy 1:3, "I thank God, whom I serve, as my ancestors did, with a clear conscience, as night and day I constantly remember you in my prayers." Spiritual leadership is a three-way relationship. It is *me* praying to *God* about *you*. I can't tell you the number of times God has given me insights as I have prayed for someone on my team, often revealing the next steps I need to take to listen, encourage, or challenge that person. Sometimes praying for others is the *last* step in a series of steps we take to grow our leaders. I encourage you to prioritize it as the *first* step.

4. Spiritual leaders challenge those they lead

Leaders cannot grow without challenge. Great leaders look at those they lead and challenge them, not because they see weaknesses but because they see potential. Mediocre leaders look at poor performance and negatively challenge the poor performer. Great leaders challenge all team members in ways that stretch their God-given abilities. Our job is to help people maximize who God has created them to be. The only way people grow is through challenge. And one of the most significant roles we can play in the lives of the leaders under our care is to provide healthy and intentional challenges. This can take the form of giving them "stretch assignments," calling them to take big risks, or inviting them to make more significant decisions in your area of ministry.

5. Spiritual leaders are good listeners

Spiritual leaders make themselves available as sounding boards, particularly in seasons when those they lead are struggling. Maybe those you lead have challenges they don't know how to solve or are discouraged about the progress of their group or team. It's in these times that leaders need to be a listening ear more than an advice giver. It's tempting to be the hero, to step in and try to solve their problem for them. But often the wisest response is to allow your leaders to talk through their own evaluation and assessment of the situation. Never underestimate the power of active listening. Clear the weeds and reflect back the key issues you hear them wrestling with. Clarify the problems. Then challenge them to think through what God may be wanting to teach them or steps he may want them to take. Pray with them about the challenge, listen to their solutions, confirm their wise decisions, and coach them in areas where they are struggling with uncertainty.

The best time to provide this type of listening and coaching is in a one-on-one meeting. You will want to meet one-on-one with each of your leaders a few times each year. Talk to your trainer or pastor about the frequency of these one-on-ones. It may vary church to church and even ministry to ministry.

When you are leading leaders, you have to think and lead differently than when you are leading team members. What do you think the leaders you are, or will be, leading want most from you?

Consider the following scenario:

Sue was just trained to be a new coach (leader of leaders) in her church. While she was excited about the opportunity to influence the five leaders who were now placed under her care, she was met with a less than enthusiastic response. Knowing the importance of building relationships with these leaders, she started out by making one-on-one contact with each one, inviting them to grab coffee over the next few weeks. But only one of four confirmed a date and time to do so. The others indicated they were busy and would get back to her. She has now been in the role for three months and finds herself very discouraged. While she does communicate with these leaders through email and occasional calls, it just seems they aren't responsive to making a connection with her and allowing her to provide the encouragement and coaching she would like to give.

What could be potential reasons Sue is getting this non-enthusiastic response?

What would you do in her situation? Why?

What challenges do you anticipate in getting others to readily respond to your leadership?

Reflect back on the five traits of a spiritual leader. Which one do you feel is your greatest strength?

Which one will be your greatest challenge? Why?

What can you do to grow in this area of greatest challenge?

An Agenda for Leading a One-on-One

Here's a five-part agenda you can use when meeting one-on-one with one of your leaders. These one-on-one sessions carry so much potential, so having an intentional and strategic objective in mind when entering into each session is vital. The strategic objective should address these five key areas: Getting *Personal*, Establishing *Priorities*, Addressing *Problems*, Drafting a *Plan*, Sharing in *Prayer*. The following "5-P" framework will provide a solid basis for your one-on-one session and incorporate all five areas:

1. Get *Personal*

Each one-on-one session needs to begin with an atmosphere of mutual trust, support, and encouragement. This can be accomplished by taking the time to discuss how the leader is doing on a personal level. How is s/he doing in her/his family life, spiritual health, and current circumstances? Also, remember the great value in celebrating spiritual and personal "wins," and take time to talk those out. Make sure you share from your own personal life as well.

Any quality mentoring relationship must involve sincere and mutual care for both individuals. A session that begins on a personal level allows you both to experience the value of soul care. Get to the "heart of the matter" on a unique and individual level before dealing with issues at the leadership level.

2. Establish *Priorities*

The next part of the session should focus on priorities. You can do this by simply asking them what their top three priorities are for their leadership at this time. As you meet, you can talk about the priority goals and how the leader is progressing toward completing them. This part of the session allows for open dialogue on the progress that the leader is making (or not making) and enables you to help them navigate the challenges and make progress toward their priorities.

3. Address *Problems*

The third part of the session is focused around addressing any problems that the leader is experiencing. Sometimes your leaders may be experiencing a problem that is not directly related to the priorities you have discussed. So use part of your one-on-one time to ask them if there are any problems they are encountering that you could help with. Often when I ask my leaders this question they will bring up challenges they are having with someone on their team, or scheduling issues that they want my opinion on, or a difficult decision they need to make but want to process with me first. This part of the agenda is not designed for you to solve their problems for them but to give them an opportunity to think through challenges on which they would like your opinion. Listening, asking the right questions, and sharing your thoughts could go a long way in helping them with the decision and ensuring they feel supported.

4. Draft a *Plan*

The fourth part of the session is for you and the leader to take a few minutes and plan together. The key here is to ask the leader what take-aways they have from your time together. It is not your goal to "assign" the action steps to the leader, but to help them create their own self-generated assignments.

5. Share in *Prayer*

The session ends by spending time praying together. You should lead in asking how you can specifically pray for them; then pray specifically and intentionally for their needs. Remember to pray for your leader between session times. It is a good idea to briefly follow up by text or a phone call with your leader to remind them you are continuing to pray for their specific needs and leadership.

Developing Character in Your Leaders

How are you doing so far? Are you intimidated by the thought of being perceived as a spiritual leader for others? Are you excited about the possibilities your maturity in Christ can bring about in the lives of others? The following gives you some concrete ways you can encourage your team to grow in their character:

▪ Initiate regular soul care conversations

Teams regularly work together to advance the gospel and impact those both in the community and in the church. We're often working shoulder to shoulder, but we're not working soul to soul. We don't know what's going on in each other's hearts, and we neglect each other's spiritual health.

In 1948, Billy Graham was doing a crusade in Modesto, California. He had a small team of guys, including Cliff Barrows, George Beverly Shea, and Grady B. Wilson. Before the evening crusade, he called them together for a soul conversation where he challenged them to return to their hotel rooms for one hour to pray and make a list of pitfalls that could ruin their ministry. An hour later they reconvened and shared their lists. As you can imagine, they listed sexual immorality, misuse of funds, criticizing the local church, exaggerating success, etc. Then they made what Cliff Barrows called "The Modesto Manifesto"—a commitment to guard against these temptations. For years, they held true to that manifesto. They aligned their character, their decisions, and their behavior with their intentions, and because of that, they built a ministry of high integrity. Billy Graham understood that integrity affects your influence. He wanted to have regular soul care conversations and hold his team to a standard of character that would keep them above reproach.

I was very fortunate because one of my early mentors in ministry was Bob Barrows, the son of Cliff. Every Tuesday, I would meet with Bob to trade accountability questions and answers. One of my favorite questions he would ask was, "Mac, how full are your emotional, spiritual, and physical tanks?" He always followed up with, "What are your next steps? What do you need to do to continue to grow in these areas?" Having regular soul care conversations developed my character over time.

■ Coach others to make courageous decisions

This goes back to our focus character trait for this module—courage. Many times, leaders face situations where they know the decision they have to make is not going to be popular, and so they make decisions based on popularity rather than integrity. But every hard decision displeases someone.

Back in the 1950s, evangelistic crusades followed the same segregation customs of the day—roping off separate areas for African Americans. In 1952 in Chattanooga, Tennessee, Billy Graham walked into the auditorium before the crusade started and saw the rope segregating the crowds. It bothered his heart so much that he personally walked over, grabbed the rope and took it down so that the crowd could integrate.

That was a bold decision, but it was the right thing to do. For some leaders, courage requires coaching. Several months ago, I was working with a young leader to process a decision he had to make. He knew what the right decision was, but he also was struggling with it because he knew his decision was not going to be popular. I challenged him to work through four questions to prepare his heart to make the courageous decision.

Question 1—*What options do you have?*
In his case, we considered two or three alternatives.

Question 2—*What are the consequences of each option?*
We thought through the upsides and downsides of each option.

Question 3—*What is the wise thing to do?*
We processed what wisdom came into play regarding his decision.

Question 4—*What's the price you will have to pay for making the right decision?*
He knew his decision would upset some people. Counting the cost first would help him be prepared.

Making character-based decisions requires courage and coaching. Listen to your leaders and coach them in how to make courageous decisions.

■ Model surrender

The best way to develop great character in others is to model great character yourself. The key is for you to be fully surrendered to Christ because only the Holy Spirit can develop Christlike character within us. When you model humility, integrity, patience, grace, and love, you will start to see those traits reflected in the leaders around you.

Again, I can turn to Billy Graham as an example. At a very young age, he felt that God was calling him into ministry and prayed: "God, I will go where you want me to go. I will do what you want me to do, and I will be what you want me to be." He reinforced that early decision repeatedly throughout his life, and that's why he had such great character.

His story reminds me of Paul's words in Galatians 2:20: "I have been crucified with Christ and I no longer live, but Christ lives in me. The life I now live in the body, I live by faith in the Son of God, who loved me and gave himself for me." When we live a life of full surrender God develops our depth of character to impact the lives around us.

Here are three questions to help you evaluate the type of character you're modeling for others around you:

- What *attitude* did I display today?
- What *behaviors* did I exemplify today?
- What *choices* did I make today?

Filter your attitudes, behaviors, and choices through those questions, and you'll have a good read of your influence on others each day. What you're modeling for your leaders today is determining your legacy tomorrow. Not only that but also what you're modeling for your leaders today is how you're marking their lives today and influencing their character tomorrow.

As I reflect on the life and legacy of someone like Billy Graham, I'm inspired. I'm inspired to be a man of character, but even more so, to be a man who raises up other leaders who are people of great character.

If you were teaching a young leader how to shape the character of the individuals on his or her team, what advice would you give them?

Put It Into Practice

Developing a new skill requires practice. Complete the following assignments to help you practice spiritual leadership.

1. Before your next meeting with your trainer, try using the 5-P agenda for a one-on-one with a friend, family member, or someone on your team.

Take note of how the individual responds, and reflect on these questions:

What did you do well?

What could you do better?

How comfortable were you leading this type of conversation?

How comfortable was the other person?

Come to your next session prepared to share your experience.

2. Think of a situation you're facing right now requiring leadership courage. Write down your thoughts now, then next time you meet your trainer, work through the four questions to process your options and come to a conclusion that you will act on.

Question 1—What options do you have?

Question 2—What are the consequences of each option?

Question 3—What is the wise thing to do?

Question 4—What's the price you will have to pay for making the right decision?

Reflect on Your Learning

Where did you grow the most in this competency?

What next step do you need to take to continue to grow
in this competency?

Meet with Your Trainer

Consistent practice can be a great beginning to sharpening a skill, but developing skill also requires processing what you learned with others. Meet with your trainer and discuss what you learned from this module.

2

Practicing Values-Based Leadership

Introduction

I have a friend who once told me, "Your values are more important than your vision." As a visionary, I wanted to take issue with him! But then, as I reflected, I realized there is a lot of truth to that statement. Vision is a dream of a preferred future, and most leaders are driven by a vision. If you don't have a vision of where you are headed, it's unlikely you will get there. It's common for leaders to cast a vision for reducing homelessness in the community, or for mobilizing a large percentage of their people to be actively engaged in discipleship, or for raising money to build a facility to help advance the mission of the church. But the way we go about this (our values) is as important as the destination itself (vision).

Values are key standards that describe the ways in which your church will behave. Values aren't *what* you do, but they impact the *way* you do things. For example, a pastor friend of mine has a value of generosity. When they built their new church facility it was built with the community in mind. Business people are invited to come into a beautiful workspace equipped with small office spaces, video conferencing capabilities, and a coffee machine, all free of charge. Organizations are invited to reserve the facility to use for their events, again all free of charge. Ask the people in the community about my friend's church and one word they use to describe it is "generous."

I've heard values described as "the way we do things around here." And, when executed consistently, these values shape the *culture* of your church. Others see these values and describe you accordingly.-

Similarly, a values-based leader is one who makes decisions based on the stated values of the church or team they serve. Their actions are consistently characterized by those values. Many leaders are unable to accomplish a strong team culture because they've never personally established deeply embedded core habits or values. And when the leader does not embody the values, it's difficult to expect the team to catch and embody those values. This prevents them from gaining the needed traction to move the ball down the field to accomplish the vision.

In this module we will focus on deepening your integrity and developing your competency of practicing values-based leadership.

Deepen Your Character: *Integrity*
Leaders are honest and demonstrate consistent character.

Develop Your Competency: *Values-Based Leadership*
Embody your values and lead in a way to create practices and patterns that reflect those values and move the team toward the common goal and vision.

Objectives:

1. Assess your ability to practice integrity and identify one specific step for growth in this area.

2. List behaviors and practices to demonstrate your church's core values in practical ways throughout the week.

3. Practice making values-based decisions at work, home, or in ministry.

4. Have a discussion with a group of leaders you work with, helping them evaluate how well they demonstrate the values of the church in their area of ministry.

 Deepen Your Character: *Integrity*

When you think of a person with integrity, you may think of someone who is consistent, honest, and truthful in their actions. To act with integrity is to do the right thing, regardless of whether or not it's acknowledged by others or convenient for you. Though we would all aspire to be such people, we can easily act selfishly and sinfully, behaving inconsistently with the person and leader we want to be. Situations can tempt us to act aggressively rather than with compassion, or to respond defensively rather than lovingly. Three particular insecurities can cause us to act without integrity: the desire to please people; the need to impress people; and the urge to protect self.

Inconsistencies in our actions damage trust with those we lead, whereas acting with integrity builds trust. None of us are perfect, of course, and we will fall short at times. But a spiritual leader who is filled with integrity is quick to confess and acknowledge shortcomings and to apologize. Such humility and authenticity enable followers to trust that you are a person of sterling character.

Scripture

As you read the following Scripture, meditate on what the author wishes to communicate, and answer the questions below. Allow the Holy Spirit to speak to you and challenge you in terms of how you can develop your integrity as a leader.

Proverbs 4:25–27

Let your eyes look straight
ahead;
fix your gaze directly before you.
Give careful thought to the
paths for your feet
and be steadfast in all your
ways.
Do not turn to the right or the
left;
keep your foot from evil.

Which of the three pressures can most likely cause you personally to not act with integrity: the desire to please people; the need to impress people; or the urge to protect self?

Which phrase from this passage do you most need to focus on in order to help you lead with greater levels of integrity? Why?

Living with integrity means talking and acting in ways that are consistent with godly character. Defining and acting on our personal values can help us act with greater levels of integrity. Write out three core values you, as a leader, try to embody in your walk with Christ.

1.

2.

3.

Now put a grade beside each value above, based on how well you think you are embodying each one.

Which value do you live out most consistently? How is that value demonstrated in your actions?

Which value do you want to improve on? What are some ways that value could be better demonstrated in your actions?

What did this exercise reveal about your integrity?

What action step do you need to take to grow in your integrity?

Having examined the character trait of integrity, we can now begin to work through the core competency for this module: **Embody your values and lead in a way to create practices and patterns that reflect those values and move the team toward the common goal and vision.**

As you read through this section, note how the character trait of integrity can undergird a leader's competency of being a values-based leader.

 ## Develop Your Competency: *Values-Based Leadership* ### Pre-Assessment

Before proceeding, complete the assessment below. In the final module of this training guide, you will retake it as a post-assessment to measure your transformation and growth regarding this competency.

The following proficiencies demonstrate mastery of this module's competency.

Grade yourself on each of these proficiencies A, B, C, D or E. Giving yourself an A+ indicates you are a model for others to follow. An E indicates no mastery.

Proficiency	Pre-Assessment
My team has clearly defined values.	
I share these values with the people I'm leading early and often.	
I approach decision-making through the grid of my values.	
I model my church's core values consistently.	

Proficiency	Pre-Assessment
I utilize a process for systematically evaluating our values.	
I do not allow challenging circumstances to alter our values.	
I am careful to celebrate successful implementation of our core values.	

Reflection Question

Describe a business, organization or church you've encountered whose values are very evident. What specific behaviors did you observe that made their values so evident?

Becoming a Values-Based Leader

The core values of your church should not be that different from your *personal* core values; they should be rooted in and in step with what Scripture teaches about what it means to be a disciple of Jesus. Do you value unity, for example? As a Christian, you most likely would say yes. As a team leader, if you choose to pursue unity and create the practices that enable unity to flourish among those you lead, you will inevitably create a culture that demonstrates unity.

Jesus was a man of personal conviction. Whenever society or situations tested his core values, he stood strong. When the cross loomed ahead, signaling the time for his earthly ministry to come to an end, the Bible says Jesus resolved to go through with it. We read in Luke 9:51, "As the time approached for him to be taken up to heaven, Jesus resolutely set out for Jerusalem." Jerusalem could only mean one thing—the place where he would be arrested and crucified. He made his decision to go to Jerusalem far in advance because of what he believed about his purpose: to save the world from sin.

When you develop personal convictions and live by a set of core values defined by the Word of God, others take note. You start to develop a reputation for what you prioritize and the way you invest your time and resources. Remember what the religious leaders said about the disciples. The Bible says in Acts 4:13, "When they saw the courage of Peter and John and realized that they were unschooled, ordinary men, they were astonished and they took note that these men had been with Jesus." Their reputation preceded them. There was no doubt what these men believed, because their actions spelled out their beliefs. They had ample opportunity to ditch their values when the going got tough—but they stood strong as men of character.

Are Your Values Adding Value?

Leaders are visionaries—they have a picture of a preferred, future reality and are passionate, enthusiastic, and optimistic about leading others to that destination. Yet, leaders can easily become discouraged or disillusioned when their God-given vision doesn't seem to gain traction. They can begin to question themselves, those they lead, and even God.

When things aren't moving forward, it can often be caused by a lack of clearly defined and integrated values. Having a clear vision doesn't necessarily mean an organization has the values to achieve that vision. Values are the engine that drives vision. They inform how a vision will become a reality. Values are much more than cute statements to hang around the office or catchy descriptions to list on a website. Values might better be described as "core behaviors" because they shape the actions of a leader and the organization they lead. In the early 2000s, I was leading my church plant to build a sports complex that would serve the community. The amount of time, energy, and money required to pull this off was bigger than any other vision I had previously led in my ministry career. The project caused me a lot of sleepless nights, and I had to navigate some conflict with church members who didn't buy into the vision. The whole thing dragged out longer than I anticipated. One of our core values as a church was "team". Doing an honest rear-view assessment, I can say that I took on too much, delegated too little, and didn't fully utilize the gifts and talents of enough people around me. Had I fully lived out the value of team, it certainly would've changed the way I led this vision and probably would've reduced some of my anxiety along the way.

A wise leader of any organization will spend significant time crafting values. He or she understands that the mission of the organization hinges on the embodiment of these traits. Sadly, in many cases these values are forgotten or ignored. As a result, the values lack the power and influence they're intended to have.

Thankfully, the values of an organization are easy to assess. All you have to do is spend time around the organization and you will quickly discern what it truly prioritizes. You are likely to hear it in the *everyday language* people use, as you'll find certain keywords and phrases have become insider language to define the core behaviors of the organization.

A few years ago, a church asked me to come for the weekend and speak to their leaders at their leadership conference. When I arrived, one of their staff picked me up from the airport, immediately thanked me, and give me an itinerary for the weekend. He then took me to my hotel where my favourite meal had been ordered from a local restaurant. That evening when I arrived to speak to the leaders, again someone escorted me, made sure I had water and snacks and was well aware of every aspect of the evening. By the time I had been there less than ten hours, I had interacted with several staff and key volunteers, and each one treated me with the utmost respect and anticipated any need I might have before I could even think of it. The next morning I was talking to the pastor and said, "By chance is one of your core values 'servanthood'?" He smiled and said, "Yes, how did you know?" I went on to explain that I had seen servanthood modeled in every interaction I had with his team. Core values are those behaviors you and your team live out consistently.

You will also see values embodied in three key ways:

1. In the *decision-making process.* Values provide a predetermined guide for decisions, and leaders will screen multiple options based on whether or not they align with their values.

2. In the *behavior* of the church. When values are effectively embodied, people will spend their time working on practices that

promote these traits, and new team members will quickly assimilate to "the way things are done around here."

3. In the *reputation* a church has in the community. A leader may *say* their church lives out particular values, but others will measure a church by its actions, not its words. It will soon have a reputation that speaks of its values—like it or not.

Imagine you were asked to teach a group of young leaders about the importance of values-based leadership. Write out three to five key points you would share with them. What illustration could you use to make your point?

Traits of a Values-Based Leader

Whether the context is a church, a corporation, or a team, values must constantly be defined and refined. This is the work of a values-based leader who is characterized by the following traits.

Trait #1: Values-based leaders model the values for their leaders.

A leader cannot lead others to certain core behaviors if they don't first embody that value themselves. Values-based leaders ooze the core behaviors they long for others to embrace. Their life communicates and reinforces the values they teach. Like Paul, these leaders can call others to follow "Whatever you have learned or received or heard from me, or seen in me" (Philippians 4:9). Paul was a living values statement, as are all values-based leaders.

Trait #2: Values-based leaders clarify the values for their leaders.

Values-based leaders know that they must help those they are leading to understand the church's values. If those you are leading don't understand or demonstrate those values, then as a team they will not behave in ways that will help accomplish the mission of the church or ministry area. Just *knowing* the values isn't enough; your leaders will need a clear understanding of what *living out* those values looks like. Will Mancini, in his book *Church Unique*, recommends creating "demonstrated by" statements for each of your values, meaning that the value must not only be stated but also matched by a corresponding metric.[1] For example, at Multiply Group,[2] one of our values is "Innovation", which is demonstrated by creating a spirit of open collaboration among the team and building feedback loops into every

1 Will Mancini, *Church Unique: How Missional Leaders Cast Vision, Capture Culture, and Create Movement* (San Francisco: Jossey-Bass, 2008), 133–34.
2 See multiplygroup.org .

service we provide in order to continue improving. Crafting values in this fashion helps leaders to act in alignment with these desired traits.

Trait #3: Values-based leaders share the values early and often.

Values-based leaders do the hard work of integrating the stated values into the life of their leaders. This process begins with bold, clear, consistent communication. When you recruit a new leader to your team, introduce them to the church's core values as quickly as possible. Tell stories of ways other leaders have demonstrated these values. Share how living out those values has impacted your own leadership. It will take time for them to retain and understand these values so be consistent and creative in the way you communicate. Columbia International University excels in this practice. Under the leadership of Dr. Bill Jones, the core values of the school are deeply entrenched in the behavior of the faculty. When I was on campus several years ago I saw why their values are so strong—each of their values is literally etched onto giant rocks located in strategic places all across the campus.

Trait #4: Values-based leaders make decisions through the grid of the values.

Leaders are prone to make decisions based on intuition, often seeming to act impulsively and without thinking. In contrast, values-based leaders stop and consider the organization's values before making any decisions—big or small. The core behaviors become a filter through which decisions are assessed. Once made, values-based leaders will overtly connect the decision with the value, so that all members of the organization can see the connection clearly. For example, I have a pastor friend who was working with his staff to plan an upcoming men's event. The ideas drifted from the overused to the mundane—wild game dinners or a speech by a semi-famous athlete. The pastor spoke up and said, "Guys, one of our values is that we make bold moves. How are any of these ideas a bold move?" After this course-correction, the staff orchestrated a cage fight night! Not only was this a bold move, but it was a perfect missional strategy for their culture, and the event was a huge success.

Trait #5: Values-based leaders systematically evaluate the values.
Most leaders are highly motivated by their vision. They can't get to their objectives soon enough. For this reason, they are often ruthless at evaluation. They assess programs, events, services, performance, and even people. If a leader is not careful, however, they may neglect to evaluate the most important factor—the organization's core values. Several years ago, I was personally discouraged by my team's lack of alignment with our stated values, so I asked each of my seven key leaders to assess our church around our six values. I gave everyone an index card and asked them to put a grade beside each value based on how well they thought we were doing at embodying it. After tabulating the results, we were able to discuss the factors that caused us to live out our highest-rated value and develop a plan to improve in those areas that scored low. This type of evaluation is necessary on a quarterly basis in order to develop a culture that revolves around the organization's values.

Trait #6: Values-based leaders stand strong for the values.
Something (or someone) will always work against your values, so values-based leaders must fight to defend them. Paul models values-based leadership in chapter 4 of his letter to the Philippians. He had received word that two ladies, Euodia and Syntyche, were at odds with each other, which ultimately could lead to division in the church. He not only urges these two women to get along, but invites others to help these women reconcile for the sake of the gospel. In a

difficult situation, Paul chose to emphasize and act upon the core value of unity (Philippians 4:1–3).

For a host of reasons, it is natural for all churches and organizations to drift away from their values. If handled maturely and wisely, leaders can leverage these "drifts" to validate and reinforce the defined values. Leaders must guard the core values and hold others accountable to working toward these, otherwise the values do not shape our team and church the way they are intended to.

Trait #7: Values-based leaders celebrate the tangible expressions of the values.

You may have heard the axiom, "What gets celebrated gets replicated." This principle is certainly true for an organization's values. Leaders must work to affirm and celebrate when they observe others living out the stated values. I once served in a church that valued discipleship. But several younger staff members seemed more intent on working to gather a big crowd to an event than engaging more people in discipleship. I couldn't understand why. Then it hit me—I was repeatedly celebrating attendance numbers in our staff meetings. These younger leaders were simply trying to accomplish the values they saw me celebrate. If we truly wanted to value discipleship, then we should have found ways to elevate this value. We should have been telling stories from the stage of people being discipled, highlighted the number of disciple-makers we had actively involved in discipling people, and acknowledged those staff and team members who were making progress toward this stated value. We needed to change what we celebrated, so that the staff's actions would follow.

There is simply no shortcut to creating a culture driven by healthy values. But given enough time, repetition, and discipline, a values-based leader can embody these traits to take proactive steps to move their team closer and closer to the God-given vision.

Who is the best values-based leader you know? What would you like to emulate about their leadership in order to become a better values-based leader?

List each of the values of your church below. (If there are no defined values, list what seem to be the top three values, based on your experience.)

Next, write "demonstrated by" statements for each describing how you can live out those values in your leadership role. Now find ways to intentionally live out one of those values at home, work, and church over the next week.

Values of my church	Demonstrated by	Challenge for the Week

Which of the seven traits in this section are you best at executing?

Which of the seven traits do you need to grow in the most? What are some ways you can do so?

Think of someone you are currently leading. How can you encourage them to better demonstrate one of the values of your church or team?

Put It Into Practice

Developing a new skill requires practice. Complete the following assignment to help you practice embodying your values and to lead in a way that creates practices and patterns that reflect those values and helps move the team toward the common goal and vision.

Write down a key decision you have to make at work, home, or in ministry and filter the decision through the core values of that particular environment. Then record how the values impacted the decision you made and how you handled the situation.

Reflect on Your Learning

Where did you grow the most in this competency?

What next step do you need to take to continue to grow in this competency?

Meet with Your Trainer

Consistent practice can be a great beginning to sharpening a skill, but developing skill also requires processing what you learned with others. Meet with your trainer and discuss what you learned from this module.

3

Bringing Out the Best in Your Leaders

Introduction

You probably already know that encouraging the people on your team can reap giant rewards of motivation, loyalty, and productivity. But you may not have given enough thought to the way you encourage others and your motives for doing so. There is a reason why Scripture mentions the principle of encouragement over fifty times: it's a powerful tool that helps people reach their potential. In this module we will focus on deepening your spirit of encouragement and developing your competency of bringing out the best in others.

Deepen Your Character: *Encouragement*

Leaders encourage others in such a way that it shapes their soul.

Develop Your Competency: *Bring out the best in others*

Learn how to bring out the best in others through encouraging and challenging them toward maximizing their strengths.

Objectives

1. Assess your ability to encourage others in a way that shapes their soul.

2. Identify specific next steps for helping one or two people better maximize their strengths.

3. Practice using the Invitation-Challenge Matrix.

4. Learn and practice how to have a strengths discovery conversation with someone on your team.

Deepen Your Character: *Encouragement*

The most effective encouragement is driven by a deep and abiding love for people. Many leaders try to be good encouragers, but if we focus simply on the activity of encouragement itself, we miss the opportunity to go deeper spiritually and to examine our motives. Why do we encourage those we lead? If we are honest, sometimes our motives are not exactly pure. We can encourage someone because we want them to like us. We may even be trying to consciously or subconsciously manipulate others so they will keep serving in a particular ministry role. Or we may encourage someone just to make ourselves look good in front of another person. But when we encourage others from an authentic spirit of love, we make it our sole intention to build up the person we encourage.

The author of Hebrews wrote to Christians who were tempted to fall away from the truth because of the suffering they were encountering. Life is often difficult. It's easy to grow discouraged, bitter, and tired … even if you are a Christian. In Hebrews 3, the author reminds the early church of the generation that followed Moses in the wilderness as they journeyed to the Promised Land. Though they had a hopeful future ahead of them, they grew weary of the conditions in the wilderness, fell into complaining and disbelief, and as a result ended up wandering in the wilderness for forty years. The author of Hebrews warns these believers not to harden their hearts as their ancestors had done but instead to "encourage one another daily" (Hebrews 3:13). He gives *encouragement* as an antidote to a hardening heart.

Encouragement is so much more than just telling someone "thank you" or "you did a good job." When done well, encouragement has the power to shape a person's soul. Words of encouragement can infuse someone with a new perspective, a new level of faith, or a new way of seeing themselves. Encouragement keeps our hearts pliable, resistant to Satan's lies, and enables us to live with a healthy perspective of God and ourselves.

Scripture

As you read the following Scripture, meditate on what the author wishes to communicate, and answer the questions over the page. Allow the Holy Spirit to speak to you and challenge you about how you can develop your character as a leader so that you encourage others in a way that shapes their soul.

Hebrews 3:12–13

See to it, brothers and sisters, that none of you has a sinful, unbelieving heart that turns away from the living God. But encourage one another daily, as long as it is called "Today," so that none of you may be hardened by sin's deceitfulness.

Who has been the biggest encourager in your life? In what ways has that person encouraged you?

What one word in Hebrews 3:12–13 stands out to you the most? Why?

Why do you think God repeatedly tells us in his Word to "encourage one another"?

On a scale of 1 to 5, how would you rate yourself as an encourager? _____

(1= I am not a good encourager at all; 2 = I try but I know I'm not good at it; 3 = I tell people I appreciate them, but don't think I am a great encourager; 4 = I am consistent in encouraging others but have room to grow; 5= I am a model others can learn from and emulate.)

Why did you give yourself that score?

What one thing could you do to become a better encourager?

Having examined the character trait of encouragement, we can now begin to work through the core competency for this module: **Learn how to bring out the best in others through encouraging and challenging them toward maximizing their strengths**.

As you read through this section, note how the character trait of being an encouraging leader can undergird a leader's competency of bringing out the best in others.

Develop Your Competency: *Bring out the Best in Others*
Pre-Assessment

Before proceeding, complete the assessment below. In the final module of this training guide, you will retake it as a post-assessment to measure your transformation and growth regarding this competency.

The following proficiencies demonstrate mastery of this module's competency.

Grade yourself on each of these proficiencies A, B, C, D or E. Giving yourself an A+ indicates you are a model for others to follow. An E indicates no mastery.

Proficiency	Pre-Assessment
The encouragement I give is sincere.	
The encouragement I give is specific.	
The encouragement I give is strengths-focused.	
I regularly and intentionally try to catch people doing things right.	

Proficiency	Pre-Assessment
I know my leaders' strengths.	
I encourage their strengths.	
I challenge them toward growth.	

Reflection Questions

What would you say is your greatest strength?

How did you come to discover this?

Bringing Out the Best In Your Leaders

Sometimes churches identify leaders, recruit and place them in a role, and pretty much leave them to it, without any ongoing equipping or encouragement. They have confidence that the individual can lead a team or a group, but often this assumption results in leaders becoming discouraged, burned out, and feeling underappreciated or under-supported.

Such leaders are often good leaders, but imagine what could happen if instead we made a good leader a *better* leader. Doing so requires giving them encouragement, providing ongoing support, and challenging them to continue to grow in their leadership. When we challenge a leader to grow in their leadership skills, there will be a trickle-down effect and the people they lead will also grow as a result.

John Maxwell's first law of leadership is "The Law of the Lid." It says, "Leadership ability is the lid that determines a person's level of effectiveness."[3] It's true. Here's what I've discovered: the better a leader gets, the bigger the impact they have. And by focusing on bringing out the best in your leaders, you can have a huge impact on your church or organization.

Let me illustrate. Imagine you are providing leadership for three leaders who report to you. Let's imagine that one of those ranks six out of ten on the leadership scale. Another is a five and the third one is an eight. As you provide coaching and encouragement to these leaders, you can begin to draw out the best in them. Over time the six grows to an eight, the five grows to a nine, and the eight also grows to a nine. Think of the cumulative impact this will have not only on their own lives but on those they lead.

For years I struggled in my leadership. In fact I had several people

---

3 John Maxwell, *The 21 Irrefutable Laws of Leadership: Follow Them and People Will Follow You* (Nashville: Thomas Nelson, 2007), chapter one.

tell me in my early twenties that I wasn't a good leader. Then, when I was twenty-seven, a pastor saw something in me that I didn't see in myself. He began to meet with me regularly—getting to know me, encouraging me, and challenging me to grow in my leadership. His investment in me radically changed my life by bringing out the best in me.

As a leader of leaders, you can have a huge impact on your church and ministry area, simply by bringing out the best in the leaders you serve. I've discovered there are three critical elements that work together to bring out the best in others:

1. *Know* their strengths;
2. *Encourage* their strengths; and
3. *Challenge* their strengths.

1. Getting to Know Their Strengths

Now, if you can't identify someone's strengths, you certainly can't encourage them or challenge them to grow in their strengths. So to help you discover the strengths of those you are leading, try this exercise the next time you meet with one of your leaders, either at work or in your area of ministry. Ask the following questions:

- Name three to four projects or goals you've been working on for the past four weeks.
- Where have you felt surges of energy during the past four weeks? What were you doing when you felt them?
- What fruit or results have you seen in the past four weeks? What are the specific things you did to contribute to that outcome?
- To what do you attribute those results? Be specific. What response have you seen from others as you did this work?
- Reverse engineer what you did well. Think about what you did well

and why. Write down the skills you used to accomplish those things.

- What do you learn about your strengths from these observations?
- What are two or three things you can put into practice over the next thirty days to sharpen that strength?

When you take someone through this process there are four outcomes:

1. They will identify their strengths.
2. They will develop their strengths.
3. They will begin to use their strengths with more intentionality.
4. They will increase their ability to develop others in that particular strength area.

Make a list of those who currently serve under your leadership, either at work or at church. Beside each name, write out what you believe to be their top strength. To what degree do you feel they are maximizing their strength?

Name	Strength	% using their strength

Whose strengths do you need to get to know better?

What specific things will you do to help you better understand
their strengths?

Looking again at the names of those who you lead, choose one
or two people. How could you help them better maximize
their strengths?

The first step towards being a good leader is to *know* the strengths of individual team members. The next step is to *encourage* them to work in those strengths. If someone is good at something and you empower them to use that strength, the organization wins and the individual wins. That's just good leadership. Let's look at ways you can encourage their strengths.

2. Encourage Their Strengths

"The mouth of the righteous is a fountain of life" (Proverbs 10:11)

We've all had that moment where we were impressed with someone's performance and felt the urge to give them a word of encouragement. Then, as soon as we open our mouth, the only thing that comes out is something like, "Hey, you did a great job tonight!" or "Thanks for your leadership. That was good today." While I'm sure they appreciate the praise, think of how much more powerful our words could be if we simply put some thought and intention into our encouragement.

Encouragement is powerful and can lift a spirit, shape self-esteem, and galvanize an individual's resolve to continue in the face of difficulty. Do your encouraging words have power, or are they just ineffectual comments? Years ago, Larry Crabb and Dan Allender wrote an entire book on this subject, called *Encouragement: The Key to Caring*.[4] An entire book on encouragement! We have much to learn about this simple yet influential leadership skill.

Perhaps the key to packing a punch to our praise is looking at the components of effective encouragement. While there is much more to

---

4 Lawrence J. Crabb Jr. and Dan B. Allender, *Encouragement: The Key to Caring* (Grand Rapids, Michigan: Zondervan, 1984).

this concept than the following explanation, let's look at three simple but potent ingredients of effective encouragement.

i. Sincerity

Before speaking words of encouragement, check your motives and make sure you're doing it to lift up the other individual, not to gain something for yourself. In Proverbs 26:28, Solomon warns us, "a flattering mouth works ruin." The Hebrew word for "ruin" comes from a root word meaning "to push, drive away, or cast down." If we're not careful, insincere words can have the opposite effect we intended, pushing people away instead of building them up.

I was having lunch with a young man one day who continued to sing my praises throughout the whole hour. Though I'm sure he wasn't an insincere person, his comments came across that way because he had never met me before that day. While I'm always up for a dose of encouragement, in this instance I found myself pulling back a little rather than being drawn to him. Encouragement is always best served in a spirit of sincerity.

ii. Specificity

If you want your words of praise to have more punch, then be specific with your encouragement. Notice the specifics of what people do well and consider how they impacted you personally. If you look closely enough, you can find little nuances that made something special.

My wife, Cindy, and I often watch the TV show *Chopped* on The Food Network. I'm always fascinated at how much detailed feedback the judges give about the look, taste, and flavors of each dish. They're able to praise or critique each chef in great detail because they've acquired a sensitive palate that enables them to taste flavors the average person doesn't notice. In the same way, we must look for and praise the specific detail of an individual's work. That kind of specificity takes encouragement to a much deeper, more meaningful level.

So instead of saying, "Hey, you did a good job," you can say something like, "When you led the small group discussion tonight, you really asked insightful questions that challenged my thinking in new ways. You have a real gift of making people think. I appreciate you using that gift to add value to my spiritual walk." Specific encouragement is meaningful encouragement.

iii. Strengths-focused

God has gifted each of us in very specific ways. Each day, we use and develop those strengths. Over time as those strengths develop and mature, they become obvious to others. The Apostle Paul had been around young Timothy so much that he became very familiar with his apprentice's strengths. And then, at a very crucial time in Timothy's ministry, Paul told him to, "fan into flame the gift of God" (2 Timothy 1:6). By centering our encouragement on someone's particular strengths, we are helping that person to fan the flame of his or her strengths. Giving sincere, specific encouragement, focused on a person's unique strengths, helps them learn something new about themselves and deepens their wisdom and insights for using that particular strength.

I've always said that encouragement is one of the most overlooked leadership development tools available to us. It is a small investment we can make daily and it reaps a huge return. Solomon observed, "A word fitly spoken is like apples of gold in a setting of silver" (Proverbs 25:11 ESV). The right word, spoken the right way, at the right time, can impact lives in ways we may never know.

Which of the three traits are you best at when you encourage someone: Sincerity, Specificity, or Strengths-focused?

Which of these three traits do you need to grow in the most?

Think of leaders in your area of ministry. What are some common discouragements they tend to face in their leadership role? Make a list below.

As you discovered in answering the previous question, leaders can face a variety of factors that lead to discouragement. And discouragement can cause a leader to stop leading and miss out on the impact God is calling them to make by using their gifts.

Imagine one of your leaders comes to you and informs you she is about to "take a break" from leading for a while. She has been leading in this particular area of ministry for a little over a year and you felt she was doing a good job in her role. When you dig into why she wants to take a break, you get a sense she is not so much tired as she is discouraged. Obviously, if God is calling her to take a break, then you mustn't stand in her way. But if a spirit of discouragement, rather than the Holy Spirit, is influencing her decision, then God can use you to help her persevere.

Considering what you learned in the first module about being a spiritual leader and what you've learned so far in this module about bringing out the best in others, what would you do to help this leader further process her decision to take a break?

3. Challenge Them to Grow Their Strengths

Great leaders not only know and encourage their people to use their strengths, they go a step further and work with others to *develop* those strengths. Escalating a strength of a team member energizes, empowers, and engages them at a whole new level. Don't just use the talent of your people: develop it. That's what this third step is all about.

I was having breakfast with a business guy the other day, and after a bit of small talk, he shared with me that he felt stuck in his leadership. I began my typical approach to this kind of discussion by asking some probing questions. As he defined the problem, I shifted to some evaluative-type questions. Next, as he began to reveal more about his situation, I took a rocket and launched a disruptive question his way. His reaction was so funny. He looked at me, then he looked away, and then looked at me again and said, "Wow, nobody's ever asked me a question like that."

I could literally see his brain cranking and going into a different mode as he considered the answer to my question. As he struggled to answer it, new thoughts, new ideas, and new insights started to explode in his mind. As a result, he came to a clear reason why he was stuck, and enthusiastically discovered the next steps he needed to take in order to overcome the challenges he was facing. Every time I've seen him since that day, he's thanked me for that conversation. He has told me so many times that our forty-minute talk changed the trajectory of his leadership.

That's not my doing—it's simply the power of disruptive questions. Unfortunately, not many leaders use this level of questions with those they lead. Merriam-Webster Dictionary defines the word "disrupt" this way: "to cause (something) to be unable to continue in the normal way, or to interrupt the normal progress or activity of (something)."

You see, when you're developing people, the thing you're fighting against is their current knowledge, their normal habits, their normal beliefs, their normal way of thinking. In order for people to really grow and transform in their leadership, there are times when we have to explode some dynamite in their thinking. In other words, we want to disrupt the normal way of thinking in order to stimulate change and growth.

Mike Breen provides a very helpful Invitation-Challenge matrix that teaches how to invite a person you are leading into your life and at the same time challenge them toward growth.[5]

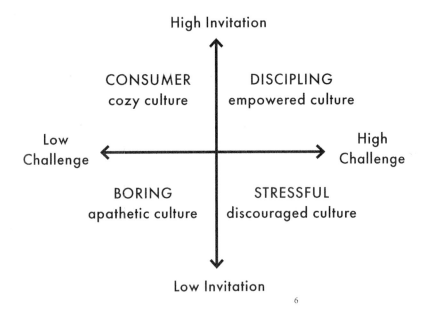

Commenting on the "discipling" quadrant of this matrix, Ben Sternke defines the challenge we issue to people this way: "An attitude that says, 'I want you to grow, I'm committed to holding you

5 Mike Breen, *Building a Discipling Culture: How to Release a Missional Movement by Discipling People Like Jesus Did,* 3rd Edition (3DM Publishing, 2017) 13–18.
6 Mike Breen, *Building A Discipling Culture,* 15. Used by permission.

accountable to change for the better."[7] Most organizations and churches struggle with an imbalance between invitation and challenge. When people feel too comfortable (low challenge), it results in stagnant growth. Conversely, too much challenge, without the comfort of an inviting and safe atmosphere (low invitation), results in discouragement.

As a leader of leaders, you probably lean toward one or the other in your leadership style. Sternke reminds us, "'Challengers' will feel like they are being overly-mushy and sentimental when they're actually calibrating an almost-appropriate amount of invitation. 'Inviters' will feel like they are being harsh task-masters when they're actually calibrating an almost-appropriate amount of challenge."[8]

Encouragement that brings with it a healthy dose of challenge is the balance we're trying to strike. Thoroughly and regularly encourage your leaders—and also challenge them to not stay the way they are but instead maximize their potential.

Consider the Invitation–Challenge matrix. Which are you better at: Invitation or Challenge?

Looking at the names you wrote in the table on page 84, what does each person need the most from you right now: Invitation or Challenge? Write an "I" or a "C" for Invitation or Challenge respectively next to their names in the table.

---

7 Ben Sternke, "How I Make Disciples: Invitation & Challenge," *Ben Sternke blog,* June 11, 2013. http://bensternke.com/how-i-make-disciples-invitation-challenge/ .
8 Sternke, "How I Make Disciples: Invitation & Challenge."

Help Your Leaders Play to Their Strengths

There are some things I'm just not good at doing. I'm not good with details, organizational communication, or follow up … just to name a few. And the truth is that regardless of how hard I try, I will still be bad at these things. Oh, I may be able to improve slightly, but these will never be my strengths. But there is a little voice in my head that tells me, "You need to be a balanced leader. You should be good at … (fill in all the weaknesses)." It's that voice that influences me to hold on to certain responsibilities instead of delegating them to someone more skilled. And when I refuse to give up the things I'm not good at, I simply wallow in my weaknesses.

Most people struggle with this same tendency, and that's why it is important you get to know the strengths of your leaders. It's easy to assume the leaders under us are confident and competent, when in reality they may have an inner voice telling them they are not a good leader. It's when they begin to doubt themselves, or even worse compare themselves to other leaders, that Satan can gain a foothold and sow a seed of discouragement that can lead to them walking away from leadership altogether. When you know your leaders, you can help combat these negative thoughts and reinforce their strengths. That's what it means to bring out the best in others. Most people tend to be blind to their strengths or underestimate the power of their own strengths. They can become so focused on their weaknesses that it hurts their leadership.

Are your leaders wallowing in weakness? Here are four ways to help them stop this destructive behavior by reminding them of these truths:

The organization deserves better. If my organization has entrusted me with a job, then they are depending on me for results.

So if I cannot deliver on the results because of a weakness, I should delegate it to someone on my team who can help.

It drains me. It's really odd, but if I spend time doing something I am good at (a strength), then it seems to give me more energy. But when I spend time doing something I'm not good at, it drains me. And when I'm drained, I can't give my best thinking and creativity to the organization.

I rob someone else of the joy of using their strengths. I cannot tell you how many times I have felt guilty delegating a task to someone because that particular task drains me ... so I assume it drains them also. But when I ask the right person to do it, they are thrilled because the task allows them to use their gifts and strengths.

I lose time. When I am operating in my weakness, a task takes me longer. So the thing that will take me four hours to complete may only take someone else one hour.

We can all focus too much on our weaknesses because our culture has told us we are supposed to be "well balanced." But the most effective leaders are actually those who are imbalanced! They know what they're good at and they do only those things.

As leaders, there are obviously some things we have to do that we may not like or even be good at. Many leaders don't like doing administrative tasks, for example, but often this is something we just have to do as a necessary part of our lives. Yes, sometimes it can be delegated, but not always. There are some things that just need to be done, and we have to learn the discipline of doing them, regardless of whether or not it's a task we enjoy.

I always tell my team that I want 80 percent of their time to be operated in their strength zone. The other 20 percent of their time is used doing the things they have to do but might not feel very competent in. I tell them they can trust God to use them, even in their weaknesses.

Ask someone to name their weaknesses, and they can typically fire off a laundry list of shortcomings without hesitation. But ask what they're good at, and many tend to struggle for an answer. People generally struggle to identify their strengths for two reasons:

1. They're embarrassed. Insecurities can keep us from admitting when we're good at something.

2. They don't recognize it as a strength. It's easy to see others' strengths, but it's not always easy to see our own. Sometimes if we're good at something naturally, we can be unaware of our skill level. A few months ago, a friend mentioned a strength he had observed in my leadership. It caught me off guard because it was something I do subconsciously and had never considered to be a strength. Because he pointed it out, I now try to develop and practice this more intentionally.

It's tempting to identify a leader's weakness and try to help them grow from a three to an eight in that area of weakness. But your time will be much better invested if you help the leader develop his or her strengths.

Look again at the names you wrote in the table on page 84. Choose one to two people and write below how you could help better maximize their strengths.

Put It Into Practice

Developing a new skill requires practice. Complete the following assignments to help you practice bringing out the best in others.

1. Before next meeting with your trainer, practice giving encouragement to at least three people. Encourage a family member, co-worker, someone on your ministry team, and/or a friend using the principles you learned in this module. Take note of how each person responds and reflect on these questions:

What did you do well?

What could you do better?

How comfortable were you giving the encouragement?

2. Choose someone from your team and lead them through a strengths conversation to help them be more aware of their strengths and how they use them.

Who did you choose? Why?

How will you structure that discussion with them?

What did you learn about helping people play to their strengths from this exercise?

Reflect on Your Learning

Where did you grow the most in this competency?

What next step do you need to take to continue to grow in this competency?

Meet with Your Trainer

Consistent practice can be a great beginning to sharpening a skill, but developing skill also requires processing what you learned with others. Meet with your trainer and discuss what you learned from this module.

4

Leading Huddles

Introduction

A group of people serving together doesn't always equate to being a "team." An effective team is a group of people who are committed to each other and are using their unique gifts in a collaborative manner to accomplish a common cause. The leader's role is to unite this group of people so that they are truly connecting with each other, enjoying each other, working together, and getting the desired results.

It's likely that you are leading teams more often than you realize. At home, you may pull family members together as a team to clean the house and prepare a meal before company comes over. At work, you may be put in charge of a team to accomplish a critical project for the organization. And in your ministry role, you will surely have a team looking to you to provide clarity, communication, and vision to accomplish the mission. As a leader of leaders, you will face the challenge of uniting a group of leaders and building them into a team. One of the best ways to unite and engage these leaders is by regular huddles. Huddles are a gathering of the people who are directly under your leadership for the purpose of encouragement and ongoing equipping. In this module you will learn how to lead a huddle in a way that unites, develops, and inspires the members to more effectively accomplish the mission.

Deepen Your Character: *Humility*

Leaders consider the needs of others above their own.

Develop Your Competency: *Leading Huddles*

Lead a huddle in a way that unites, develops, and challenges members to more effectively lead their team/group.

Objectives

1. Assess where pride may be influencing your leadership and relationships.

2. Practice leading one or more elements of the Huddle Agenda and receive feedback.

3. Engage someone in conversation and use one of the 5-Hat follow-up question techniques.

4. Capture key insights for leading a huddle by watching your trainer or another person lead a huddle for leaders.

Deepen Your Character: *Humility*

When you move into a new leadership position, you will undoubtedly face the temptations of pride, power, and prestige. In fact, every time you are given more responsibility, these temptations escalate. We have to understand the power of humility to combat these temptations and keep us from falling into their traps. Demonstrating a lifestyle of humility is one of the strongest ways we can model Christlike character.

Jesus laid down all his rights as the Son of God. He did not throw his weight around and insist on special treatment. Instead, he put others above himself. When we follow Jesus' example, people will not only learn leadership competencies from us, but they will also learn the character of a true leader.

Jim Collins, in his classic book *Good to Great*, looked at a study of 1,500 Fortune 500 companies over a thirty-year period. He selected the top companies that outperformed the others to know how they sustained their success over the long term. His research noted that humility was an underlying characteristic of the leadership in those companies.[9]

Whenever we lead a meeting, such as a huddle, the temptation is to demonstrate our authority, our wisdom, and our experience. But huddles are not a time to selfishly validate our identity. They are a time for you as a leader to create a collaborative environment that elevates the collective genius of the group. The spirit of teamwork is best held together by a common spirit of humility among team members. Remember, humility and pride are equally contagious. Team members catch the spirit of collaboration and unity when the leader sets that tone. But if the leader exhibits a spirit of pride, it can actually create competition and disunity among group members. I think we've all been in situations where a colleague or peer brags about his or her accomplishments. Something within us then wants to reciprocate, to name-drop, and share our own stories of success as well. Pride repels people from a leader. Humility draws the entire group together toward a common goal.

Scripture

As you read the following Scripture, meditate on what the author wishes to communicate, and answer the questions below. Allow the Holy Spirit to speak to you and challenge you as a leader about how you can develop your character so that you practice true humility in your everyday life.

---

9 James C. Collins, Good to Great: *Why Some Companies Make the Leap and Others Don't* (New York City: HarperBusiness, 2001), chapter five.

Philippians 2:5–8

In your relationships with one another, have the same mindset as
Christ Jesus:
Who, being in very nature God,
       did not consider equality with God
           something to be used to his own
           advantage;
rather, he made himself nothing
       by taking the very nature of a servant,
       being made in human likeness.
And being found in appearance as a man,
       he humbled himself
       by becoming obedient to death—
           even death on a cross!

Think of a leader you know whose humility attracts others to follow
him or her? What do you learn from their example?

What part of your personality makes it sometimes difficult for you to demonstrate humility?

Paul tells us Jesus took on the nature of a servant. Thinking back to the Gospels, when was a time you recall Jesus demonstrating servant leadership? What impact did that action have in the moment?

Take some time to evaluate how well you are developing in the area of humility. Admittedly, our levels of humility and pride are easier for others to see in us than for us to see in ourselves. You may therefore find it helpful to invite a close friend to do this exercise with you and ask for their input.

Remember, humility is a situational character quality for most people. It's easier to be humble in certain circumstances and more difficult in others. Using the following "Humility Meter," rate yourself in the following situations by placing a mark on the line between pride and humility to represent your current attitude:

At work

Pride - - -- - - - - - - - - - Humility

At home with family

Pride - - -- - - - - - - - - - Humility

Among friends you know really well

Pride - - -- - - - - - - - - - Humility

Among peers you don't really know well

Pride - - -- - - - - - - - - - Humility

When executing a leadership role

Pride - - -- - - - - - - - - - Humility

In what area do you most consistently demonstrate humility?
Why do you think this is the case?

Looking at some of the lower scores, write down one way
you can practice humility this week.

Having examined the character trait of humility, we can now begin to work through the core competency for this module: **Lead a huddle in a way that unites, develops, and challenges members to more effectively lead their team/group**.

As you read through this section, note how the character trait of humility can undergird a leader's competency of leading a huddle.

 ## Develop Your Competency: *Leading Huddles*
Pre-Assessment

Before proceeding, complete the assessment below. In the final module of this training guide, you will retake it as a post-assessment to measure your transformation and growth regarding this competency.

The following proficiencies demonstrate mastery of this module's competency.

Grade yourself on each of these proficiencies A, B, C, D or E. Giving yourself an A+ indicates you are a model for others to follow. An E indicates no mastery.

Proficiency	Pre-Assessment
I regularly ask follow-up questions.	
I lead a huddle with high intentionality and accomplish intended objectives.	
I create a sense of community among a group of leaders.	
I facilitate discussion that leads to discovery.	

Proficiency	Pre-Assessment
I encourage and challenge leaders in the context of the huddle meeting.	

Reflection Question

What is your favorite and least favorite part of meetings?

Why?

Leading Huddles

So what is a huddle? A huddle is a gathering of a team of three to twelve people meeting for the purpose of encouragement, equipping, and empowerment in order to accomplish a specific mission. Typically, an effective huddle has five objectives: Connection, Celebration, Coaching, Communication, and Care. This gathering is not just an

ordinary meeting; it's a strategic way of providing ongoing development for your existing leaders.

Often, we think of discipleship as a gathering of one to three people
being equipped by an experienced believer—this model provides an
ideal way to prepare and develop a potential leader for a new role in
leadership. It gives a potential leader the opportunity to observe an
experienced leader in action, and to be given small assignments so
they can try their hand at leading and then receive feedback.

But I've discovered that *ongoing* discipleship/development with
your existing leaders is very effective in a larger group setting. Huddles provide an opportunity for a team to hear what God is doing in
each of their lives and enable them to learn from each other's leadership styles and experiences. Your role is not to be a teacher but to
facilitate a discussion among the group, leading to discoveries that
enable each individual to grow in their leadership.

We see Jesus frequently using a huddling technique with his disciples. For example, in Luke 9, Jesus gave his disciples a debrief after
he sent them in pairs to share the gospel throughout Galilee. This
debrief was just as important as the mission itself.

We also see Jesus using a huddle strategy in Matthew 16 when he
took his disciples to Caesarea Philippi, north of where they lived in
the Galilee area. In this setting far from home, he asked them a question: "Who do people say the Son of Man is?"(Matthew 16:13). Together they discussed all the theories of who Jesus was. Then he asked
a more vital question: "Who do *you* say I am?" (Matthew 16:15, my
italics). After they discussed his identity and listened to each other,
Jesus proceeded to give them some powerful insights about the church.

This is the pattern we see over and over in the Gospels—Jesus
huddling with his team in private moments so they could learn and
grow as leaders together. We can do the same. Each week, those we

lead encounter different situations and experiences that require feed-back and debriefing. A small group leader may be struggling to recruit new people to her group. A student leader may be baffled with how to handle a difficult person disrupting their group. A children's ministry leader may need to process how to deal with an overprotective parent. Each of these circumstances present an opportunity to debrief as a team, helping individuals further develop the leadership skills and character required in such challenging situations. Any struggle—and even a success—is a ripe learning opportunity, not just for the person involved but for all the leaders under your care. Remember, those you lead are constantly experiencing struggles and successes that you can dissect and capitalize on for the whole group to learn from.

How to Lead a Huddle

I've been using the following huddle-based techniques for years with all kinds of teams. Huddles are a powerful way to build team unity, capitalize on collaborative learning, and develop people in their leadership character and competencies. As I lead teams, huddles have become an integral part of my strategy because they serve as an excellent vehicle to unite a team and, over time, help each of us learn to live and lead more like Jesus.

Let's start with a simple five-part agenda to use when leading any huddle.

 ## 1. Connect (5–10 minutes)

This time may be as little as five minutes. Toss out an easily answered question to get people talking and break the ice. "What was the highlight of your weekend?" "What's something fun you've done with your kids recently?" "What is your favorite coffee shop in town and why?" The objective is just to connect relationally as a team and get to know each other better on a personal level. Sometimes I keep the questions casual. Other times I make them more personal: "What has God shown you in his Word in the last week?" Or "In thirty seconds or less, what is the freshest thing God has said to you recently?"

 ## 2. Celebrate (3–5 minutes)

Once again this does not take a lot of time. This slot on the agenda may be three to five minutes, and not everyone has to answer. You simply ask, "Since the last time we met, what is something we've seen God do that we can celebrate?" The objective is to celebrate what God has been doing in your life, work, or ministry. And while this doesn't take much time, it can add great value. You're not looking for everyone to give an answer. Aim for one or two people to answer so you can genuinely celebrate some wins and see God at work.

 ## 3. Coach (30–45 minutes)

The coaching portion of the agenda may last thirty to forty-five minutes. The objective is to sharpen a certain leadership competency by learning from one another's experiences, as well as from short content you provide to kick off the coaching time. You can access free huddle outlines at www.maclakeonline.com/huddles. There you will find both long and short huddle outlines you can use with your teams. There are also two sample huddle outlines at the back of the book. But first, let me show you the key to making questions really work for you. When I lead a huddle, I always have this framework in mind.

Content—This is a short form of content participants read or watch to stimulate their thinking about the topic at hand. It may be reading a short article or Scripture passage or watching a short video teaching together.

Discovery—Next, we enter what I call the Discovery Zone. This is a long block of time where I am asking questions. My goal is not just to prompt good discussion. My goal is discovery. I want team members discovering new insights and ideas for growth. I ask good questions and get people thinking. During this time, I don't want to be the expert in the room who gives all the answers. I want them to discover truths—not just hear me deliver truths. When this is working really well, you will notice that your leaders begin to ask questions; they start to dig deeper because their curiosity is piqued and their desire to grow has increased. Near the end of the allotted time, I may take more of a directive role and will introduce specific content I have prepared. But I wait until the end to insert most of my insights and thoughts. Remember these principles of leading a group in discovery:

i. *Bite your tongue*—Don't let silence bother you. Focus on their processing and thinking.

ii. *Be curious*—Curiosity will cause you to ask good follow-up questions. For example: "Why do you think that?" "How would you apply that?" "How have you seen that work in the past?" (See the section on page 119, "Ask effective follow-up questions" for more guidelines on this.)

iii. *Be challenging*—Ask good, open-ended questions that you would enjoy answering. Do not ask questions with obvious yes/no answers.

As you wrap up the coaching segment, always end the time by asking everyone to write down and share what next step they will take to grow in the area of character or competency discussed.

Asking each of your team to think of a tangible next step to apply what they have learned is essential if they are to see transformation in their character and/or competencies. Many times I will make a note of, or ask them to submit, their action steps, so I can follow it up in a one-on-one. Or, sometimes I add a "check-up" section at the beginning of a huddle, giving opportunity for individuals to feed back on how well they managed to carry out their action steps from the previous huddle.

 ## 4. Communicate (1–3 minutes)

This portion of the meeting is only one to three minutes. The object-ive is to make sure everyone knows about any important upcoming events or dates. At this point, you can let them know about the date and time of your next huddle, details about important events coming up, or logistical information about their area of ministry they need to be aware of.

 ## 5. Care (10–15 minutes)

Make sure you save time to ask, "How can we pray for each other?" Spend a few minutes praying with and for each other. This step active-ly invites God into the process and allows your team to connect soul to soul, deepening their connection with each other.

How would you describe your confidence level on a scale of 1–5 in leading a huddle as described in this module: 1 – I am not confident, 3 – I am somewhat confident, 5 – I am highly confident? If you scored 1 or 2, what is your biggest concern in leading huddles? If you scored 3, what area do you need to grow in the most to increase your confidence level? If you scored 4 or 5, what strength do you bring to leading huddles?

What common mistakes do you think huddle leaders make? Which of those do you fear you will be guilty of making?

Huddle Nuts and Bolts

Frequency and Duration of Huddles: How Often Should You Meet? How Long for?

Depending on the type of team you lead, there are two factors you have to consider: frequency and duration.

Frequency—This all depends on how much your team needs to connect. For some teams this may be once a month. Others may need to meet every other month or once a quarter.

Duration—For some teams it may be a short huddle—ten to twenty minutes. (See the huddle sample at the end of the book for suggested timings for a shorter huddle.) Other teams will need to meet for sixty to seventy-five minutes.

For example, children's ministry may want those leading their leaders to meet with the leaders once a month in a short huddle. Small group ministry may want their leader of leaders (often times called a "Small Group Coach") to meet with small group leaders once a quarter for a long huddle. The frequency and duration will vary ministry to ministry.

Best Practices of Effective Huddles

Adhering to the following best practices of highly effective huddles can help you avoid mistakes that others have learned the hard way. Applying what you learn here will save you time in preparation and will also help ramp up your productivity.

• *Help members participate in discovery not just discussion*

A couple of years ago I was leading a huddle session with a small cohort of church planters. We were discussing an important aspect of their leadership as church planters. I started asking one of the guys a series of questions to help him think deeper on the topic. I'd ask and he'd answer. I'd ask again and he'd dig deep and answer again. I continued to ask him a series of questions until he finally looked at me and said, "Oh, man, my head hurts! Can you just tell me the answer?" I smiled and explained that if I gave him the answer, I would rob him of the opportunity to discover truth for himself.

So often we rush to tell people what we know. Perhaps it's because we don't like to watch them struggle or we don't enjoy the time it takes to lead someone through self-discovery. Or perhaps it's because we like others to see how smart we are! When I was a student at Dallas Theological Seminary, Dr. Howard Hendricks, my favorite professor and well-known educator in his field, would often give us challenging assignments and ask us challenging questions. Then he would say, "Are you sufficiently frustrated?" When we would let out a collective cry of "Yes!" he would reply, "Good, you're learning." Making people wrestle with questions is essential to the learning process.

• **Keep the focus on equipping members to live a biblical lifestyle of leadership**
In the church, we are often solely concerned about teaching people to turn our ministry widgets, rather than really equipping them to lead like Jesus in every area of their lives—in their work, home, and church context. Sometimes leaders complain, "No one is attending my training huddles." If this is our reality, we have to look at what value we are delivering through our huddles. I've discovered that people appreciate what adds value to their lives. Remember, you are leading people, not just an agenda, so you want participants to walk away from huddles feeling they have grown in ways that will impact the way they lead in all contexts of their life, not just their church context.

• As huddle leader, don't try to be the expert in the room

Effective huddles are focused more on generating peer-to-peer learning than hearing from an expert. One of the biggest mistakes we can make in leading huddles is to take the role of teacher and talk too much. We must recognize that the leaders in the room have experience we can draw from, and our role is to help draw out that experience so they can learn from each other. I was once consulting with a group of seven key leaders and explained the importance of huddles for the purpose of ongoing development. To emphasize the fact that they could learn from each other, I asked each individual in the room how many years of leadership experience they had. The seven people had a combined total of eighty-three years of leadership experience! Then I looked at them and said, "I can take any leadership topic, and I guarantee you can learn something from each other through a simple thirty to forty-five minute discussion." Huddles are a great way of putting children's ministry leaders together and letting them learn from each other. Get your small group leaders, worship leaders, missional community leaders, or your student ministry leaders together in a huddle and let them exchange ideas and insights. If you do this, I guarantee you will see your volunteer leaders grow.

• As huddle leader, drive the team to take the next steps

The point of the huddle time together isn't just getting good ideas, facilitating a Bible study, or learning some principles. The point is to walk away with at least one action step each person can apply to grow in his or her leadership skills. At the end of the coaching portion of the agenda, ask each member to share his or her action steps. Next time you huddle, follow up by asking how they did with these steps, or you can ask about their progress in individual one-on-one settings.

Write down some of the topics you think the leaders in your area of ministry would want to grow in (e.g., soul care, delegating responsibility, handling difficult people, etc.).

Imagine you have been leading huddles every other month for eight months now. One of your leaders has not shown interest in the huddles and has only attended one out of the four you've led. What excuses might that leader give for not attending?

How would you counteract those excuses?

What would you do to encourage this leader to engage with regular huddles?

• *Ask effective follow-up questions*

As leaders, we have to ask not only great questions but great follow-up questions. I've discovered there are five types of follow-up questions that can not only generate great discussion but also meaningful discovery as well.

Here's how it works.

■ *Ask a question and listen for trigger words*

After asking one initial question, I listen to the group or individual's answer. I am listening for "trigger words" in their response that help me choose which follow-up question I want to ask.

Here's a sample script:

Huddle Leader: "What would you say is your greatest leadership strength?"

Member: "I am not sure. I've been told I am a good communicator. But other people say I am really good at organizing things. To tell the truth, I've never taken the time to find out my greatest strength."

Trigger words I hear: *communicator, organizing things* (administration), *not sure*.

■ *Ask a good follow-up question*

Now, given those trigger words, imagine putting on a different "hat" that represents five types of question. Choose from the following list:

 1. Fisherman—Point of View question

Ask for the person's perspective or point of view in order to discover opportunity or obstacles. From the example above I might choose the trigger words "not sure" and ask a Fisherman question: "Why do you think you have a hard time identifying your strengths?"

 2. Reporter—Story question

Draw out a story from the person's past experience on the topic in order to discover a leadership insight. From the example above, I could choose the trigger word "communicator" and ask a Reporter question: "You said someone told you that you were a good communicator. Take us back to that moment; what prompted them to tell you this, and did they give you any specific feedback about your communication?"

3. Physician—Self-Assessment question

Ask the individual to diagnose themselves in order to discover their strengths or weaknesses. From the example above, I could choose the trigger word "communicator" and ask a Physician question: "On a scale of 1–5, with 5 being high, how would you describe your skill level in communication? Why did you choose [insert number they chose]? What do you need to do to grow to a [insert one number higher than they chose]?"

 4. Contractor—List Building question

Ask the individual or group to identify a list or framework to discover different perspective or insights. From the example above, I could choose the trigger words "not sure." I could ask a Contractor question: "What are five reasons that tend to cause people to be unaware of their primary strengths?"

 5. Pilot—Action Step question

After a member has identified something to work on, ask the individual to identify a flight path—practical next steps that will guide them in the direction of growth and development. From the example above, I could choose the trigger words "administration" and "communication" and ask a Pilot question: "What three action steps could you take that will help you discover if administration or communication is your primary strength?"

Which of the five types of follow-up question do you use most often or most naturally in conversation with others?

Which one(s) will you try to implement more often as a result of reading this module? Explain.

Leading huddles can be an extremely rewarding experience. Helping those you lead to grow will have a huge impact on the mission of your ministry. Put the principles above into practice and you will discover that your leaders will look forward to the next huddle because of the investment it brings into their lives.

Put It Into Practice

Developing a new skill requires practice. Complete the following assignments to help you practice the various aspects of the competency of leading huddles.

1. Observe your trainer or someone else leading a huddle. Note your observations here and prepare to share them with your training group. And/ or lead a portion of a huddle under the guidance of your trainer. After the huddle, discuss with your trainer what you did well and what you could've done better.

2. Practice active listening among a small group of friends by using each of the "Five Hats" follow-up questions. Write down what you learned from that experience.

3. Study the huddle examples at the back of the book and use them as a guide to create your own huddle session. Bring a copy of your huddle session to your next training to share with your trainer and the others in your training group.
(Get access to more huddles at www.maclakeonline.com/huddles)

Reflect on Your Learning

Where did you grow the most in this competency?

What next step do you need to take to continue to grow in this competency?

Meet with Your Trainer

Consistent practice can be a great beginning to sharpening a skill, but developing skills also requires processing what you learned with others. Meet with your trainer and discuss what you learned from this module.

5

Recruiting New Leaders

Introduction

Great ideas rarely become reality without a great team. Leaders are never short on vision, but without a skilled team to execute their God-given dream, nothing happens, or if something does happen, it all depends on one person. In this module, you will discover the keys to getting the right people engaged in the vision and recruiting them to a team.

There will be times when God may give you the opportunity to lead a cause at work, with your family, or in your community, where you will need a team of people using their gifts to accomplish the goal. Your ability to identify, recruit, and mobilize the right people will be crucial to the success of that mission. The principles discussed in this module apply to all contexts, whether you are mobilizing help for your little league baseball team, planning a family reunion, or recruiting a team for your area of ministry. Remember, a small start can lead to something great. Influencing someone to take on a small task today may build their confidence to step into leadership tomorrow. Encouraging a person to take a next step today may lead to taking a bold step in a greater mission for Christ tomorrow.

Deepen Your Character: *Passion*

Leaders are filled with a fervent drive toward the cause God has given them.

Develop Your Competency: *Recruiting Leaders*

Expand your team by following a deliberate recruitment process.

Objectives

1. Assess your passion in your daily relationship with God.

2. Observe and learn from watching another leader recruit someone into a ministry role.

3. Assess your ability to recruit others following a deliberate process.

4. Identify next steps to help you grow in your competency of expanding your team by following a deliberate recruitment process.

Deepen Your Character: *Passion*

When I'm close to God, I'm more passionate about the mission of God. Unfortunately, the opposite can also be true; when I've lost some of my zeal for intimacy with the Father, I start to lose passion for his work. It feels like pushing a rock uphill. There are also times when my work for God can cause me to burn out in my relationship with him. And that's when ministry gets tough. Being in tune with God creates a desire within me to accomplish the vision he has given me as a leader. And God can use that passion to attract others to that vision. I've discovered over many years of ministry that as God burdens my heart around a specific cause, he then begins to draw people around me. God loves community, and I can only imagine how he smiles as we engage and empower others in the vision, rather than trying to do it all ourselves.

No passion for God? No passion for his work. No one is going to follow your leadership.

My friend Vance is fond of reminding leaders, "Our primary calling is not to ministry but to intimacy." Are you frustrated by your progress in recruiting others to join you in God's work? The answer is not to work harder but to draw closer. Galatians 6:9 exhorts us, "Let us not become weary in doing good, for at the proper time we will reap a harvest if we do not give up." Intimacy with the Father is essential to maintaining a healthy passion for his work. Scripture reminds us to work with our whole heart (Colossians 3:23). God wants us to have a heart that's on fire for him. Not our work. Not our ministry. Solely for him.

Scripture

As you read the following Scripture, meditate on what the author wishes to communicate, and answer the questions below. Allow the Holy Spirit to speak to you and challenge you as a leader about how you can develop your character in this area of being more passionate in your calling.

Colossians 1:28–29

He is the one we proclaim, admonishing and teaching everyone with all wisdom, so that we may present everyone fully mature in Christ. To this end I strenuously contend with all the energy Christ so powerfully works in me.

Who do you know who has a passion for Christ you admire?

What do you learn from their example?

When you read Paul's words in Colossians 1:28–29, what would you like to emulate from his example?

What factors are either fueling or extinguishing your passion for God at this time?

If we're honest, there are times when we have more passion for God than others. The best way to grow your passion is to start with an honest assessment of where you are presently. Imagine your passion for intimacy with God as a flame. Which of the following three pictures best illustrates your level of passion for intimacy with God right now?

Why did you choose that picture?

Write down one insight this exercise reveals about you.

What one action step could you take to grow in this area?

Having examined the character trait of passion, we can now begin to work through the core competency for this module: **Expand your team by following a deliberate recruitment process**.

As you read through this section, note how the character trait of passion can undergird a leader's competency of recruiting others.

 **Develop Your Competency:**
Recruiting Leaders
Pre-Assessment

Before proceeding, complete the assessment below. In the final module of this training guide, you will retake it as a post-assessment to measure your transformation and growth regarding this competency.

The following proficiencies demonstrate mastery of this module's competency.

Grade yourself on each of these proficiencies A, B, C, D or E. Giving yourself an A+ indicates you are a model for others to follow. An E indicates no mastery.

Proficiency	Pre-Assessment
I give potential recruits time to pray about the decision.	
I tell the individual why I chose him or her.	
I ensure his or her gifts and passions fit the position.	
I provide a written description of expectations.	

Proficiency	Pre-Assessment
I make sure he or she observes and shadows a veteran volunteer.	
I provide adequate training for the position.	
I follow up within thirty days after recruiting a new person.	

Reflection Question

What was the best volunteer role you've ever had?

Why?

Recruiting Leaders

Think of a time you said "yes" to an opportunity to serve. What factors encouraged you to agree to the commitment? Perhaps we can learn something from a leader named Nehemiah. He took on a tough assignment, bordering on the impossible, and yet received an enthusiastic "yes" from a group of volunteers when he recruited them. If anyone had a reason to be skeptical about getting involved, it would be the people of Jerusalem. Their enemy had destroyed the wall years earlier, and after several failed attempts at rebuilding it, they had developed an apathetic attitude. Nehemiah, however, faced the challenging task of rebuilding with great zeal.

Nehemiah 2:17–18 tells the story:

> Then I said to them, "You see the trouble we are in: Jerusalem lies in ruins, and its gates have been burned with fire. Come, let us rebuild the wall of Jerusalem, and we will no longer be in disgrace." I also told them about the gracious hand of my God on me and what the king had said to me. They replied, "Let us start rebuilding." So they began this good work.

One of the reasons Nehemiah was enthusiastic was because he'd already seen God do a great work. Earlier in chapter two, we see that the heathen king of Persia had released Nehemiah to return to Jerusalem to build up the walls. God had clearly moved in the heart of this king to enable Nehemiah to leave, and it had no doubt bolstered Nehemiah's faith. Emboldened, Nehemiah made a big move with a huge "ask." How did he get the people of Jerusalem to commit?

There are four essentials we must keep in mind when recruiting:

1. Begin with prayer

In chapter one of the book of Nehemiah, we see Nehemiah wrestling in prayer, passionately seeking God. God placed this burden on Nehemiah's heart and through prayer guided him to a strategic approach to rebuild the wall. That strategic approach included recruiting the king of Persia to help resource the project, garnering the support of key leaders in Jerusalem, and mobilizing the people in strategic locations to rebuild portions of the wall. This big vision required a big team of people.

When Cindy and I were called to plant a church in Myrtle Beach, South Carolina I immediately begin to study church planting. Again and again I heard the same wisdom from different church planters: "Start praying and fasting now for the people God wants to bring around you to help reach your community." So months before we held our first official interest meeting, we had a list of names that God had put on our hearts—people we were praying for and would eventually invite to be a part of our mission. I'm thankful for that wisdom because I know how easily and how often I can run forward with a vision and neglect praying for those God wants to be involved.

2. Recognize the work is God's work

There is no doubt that Nehemiah felt a great sense of ownership of the vision of rebuilding the wall. But he knew that this was God's work. He wasn't just inviting the people into a good idea that he had. He wasn't trying to get a bunch of people to join in on his agenda. No, he knew this was God's vision and God's work.

There are times we can get so wrapped up in our ministry that we forget that this is God's work. And when we neglect this important truth, we can find ourselves recruiting people to join us, rather than join God.

3. Do your homework

Nehemiah did his homework. In chapter two, he gives an account of
some of his research:

> By night I went out through the Valley Gate toward the
> Jackal Well and the Dung Gate, examining the walls of
> Jerusalem, which had been broken down, and its gates,
> which had been destroyed by fire. Then I moved on toward
> the Fountain Gate and the King's Pool, but there was not
> enough room for my mount to get through; so I went up the
> valley by night, examining the wall. Finally, I turned back
> and reentered through the Valley Gate.
>
> Nehemiah 2:13–15

Nehemiah was doing a thorough investigation of the damage to
the wall so that by the time he invited the people to join him in the
rebuilding project he knew what he was dealing with.

It can be discouraging to a potential volunteer to say "yes" and
then find out they are walking into disorganized chaos. That's what
some of my new volunteers experienced when I was a young pastor. I
invited everyone to a work day where we would show up at a facility
and spend the day clearing, repairing, and landscaping. I was young,
passionate, and this was a great cause. But I had not done my homework. As people arrived to serve, they quickly discovered my lack of
preparation. People were standing around, unsure what to do. Some
of the tools and supplies we needed were not available, and I forgot to
provide snacks and water for those serving on a long hot day. Need-
less to say, people didn't have a great experience. We got some things
done but it wasn't fun, efficient, or unifying as a team.

It's important to invite volunteers into a clearly defined,

organized, and well-researched environment. This creates a better experience for all those involved.

4. Cast a big vision

We don't know exactly what Nehemiah said as he stood before the people; he left out the details. But he does tell them his God story: "I also told them about the gracious hand of my God on me and what the king had said to me" (Nehemiah 2:18). He told them about what God laid on his heart, the vision for rebuilding the wall and restoring their security and dignity. He told them how God had even moved the heart of the Persian king to contribute to the rebuilding of the wall. Whatever he shared certainly mobilized the crowd because they responded with an enthusiastic, "Let us start rebuilding" (Nehemiah 2:18). They began this good work.

What are you communicating when you ask someone to join your team? This is a really important question because what you're communicating both verbally and non-verbally could determine if you get a "yes" or a "no" response.

- Posting a handwritten sign on the children's ministry door that says, "Volunteers NEEDED!" communicates: "There's a problem behind these doors."

- Announcing from the pulpit, "We don't have enough volunteers in our student ministry, so please sign up to help today" communicates: "We are desperate."

- Approaching someone with, "No one's volunteering to lead around here; would you be interested?" communicates: "Something is broken in this organization."

None of these invitations are casting vision; they are announcing that disaster looms ahead! People want to be a part of something meaningful. They want to use their gifts to make a difference. When recruiting people into a position, we must cast a vision for the difference they can make by using their gifts.

Which of the four essentials above is your strength?

Which of the four do you need to grow in the most?

What was your biggest takeaway from this section?

Relationship Plays an Important Role in Recruiting

A common misconception among staff, as well as the average church member, is that the staff team is solely responsible for recruiting new leaders. This mentality is concerning because it limits recruitment efforts and creates a shortage of leaders in the church.

One of the biggest factors for getting new people into leadership is their relationship to the person making the ask.

Do you remember your first invitation into leadership? I do. Marjorie Willis, my high school English teacher, asked me to consider leading the Christian Club on campus. Why she chose me I'll never know. I was the shyest kid in the entire school, but something prompted her to ask me. Because I had a close relationship with her, I agreed to pray about it. If anyone else had asked me to step out of my comfort zone, I would have told them a definitive "no." Over the next couple of weeks, her voice of encouragement guided me to a place where I could not deny that God was calling me into that leadership role. And so I said "yes."

- I said "yes" because I believed in the fact that she believed in me.
- I said "yes" because I knew she would walk alongside me and coach me.
- I said "yes" because God knew it was her voice I would respond to more than any other.

There are potential leaders in your church who will not respond to your invitation to lead, but they would consider the task if the invitation came from a trusted friend. I've learned that people who may not respond to my voice will respond to another's. Many people mistakenly think that when Jesus called Peter and Andrew to "follow him" he recruited them the day he met them. However, it's more than likely he had known these men for some time and had observed their character and potential. By the time he said, "Follow me," it wasn't a haphazard, thoughtless invitation. No, he would have known these men, known details about their lives, and had discussions with them about their faith.

The importance of a leader's influence on others cannot be overstated. Jesus had a relationship with the twelve disciples that enabled them to grow. The greater the relationship, the greater the influence he had on them. As leaders, we must remember that people want to be known, appreciated, and valued. When people know we value who they are and that we want to see their gifts maximized, then we have a greater ability to influence their lives. When we recruit others onto a team or to a cause, it shouldn't be for our sake. When we invite others to join our team, it is a form of serving them, helping them expand who they are and maximizing the impact their lives can have for the kingdom.

Can you imagine what could happen if we empowered the voices of all our leaders to call others into leadership? *Empowering others unleashes an army of leadership recruiters that keeps our leadership pipelines consistently full of growing leaders.*

Imagine your church and area of ministry just experienced a sudden growth spurt. The pastor announces at a small gathering of leaders that he needs all your help in recruiting new leaders to help with this new growth. It's determined that you need to recruit four new leaders in your area of ministry. They would like to have these new leaders in place within the next two months.

What challenges do you think you would face recruiting these
four new leaders?

What are some of the things you would do over those two months
to recruit in a relational way?

Getting others to say "yes" to our recruitment request requires a
degree of leadership influence. Make a list of reasons people say
"yes" and a list of reasons people say "no" to volunteer service
opportunities.

Recruiting and Keeping Leaders

If we are honest, we have to admit that many recruiting efforts in churches are poorly executed because indiscriminate pleas are made out of a sense of desperation. Others can sense when we will settle for any warm bodies we can find. It's as if we wave a white flag and ask people to please get on board a sinking ship. People are attracted to momentum, and they like to be part of winning teams.

Below are seven key steps for successfully recruiting a committed leader and making it a positive experience for him or her:

1. Ensure the individual's gifts and passions fit the position you're offering

Having the wrong person in a position is just as ineffective as having no one in the position. Be patient and let God lead you to the right person with the right gifts. When we recruit the wrong person to the wrong position, we not only do the overall goal a disservice, we also do that individual a disservice.

2. Tell the individual why you thought of him or her for this role

Be very specific. The initial recruitment moment is your first chance to cast the vision to the potential candidate. Take the opportunity to develop a picture of how this person's gifts, passion, and personality match up with God's vision for that particular cause. Help the recruit see the potential for significant impact. Remember, your job is not just to fill a position but also to cast a vision.

3. Give the potential recruit time to pray

Never ask someone to make a decision on the spot. When we do "on the spot" recruiting, the individual feels the pressure to say "yes" to you, rather than truly having the opportunity to say "yes" to God. Once you make the proposal, tell the person you'd like him or her to take a few days to pray about the opportunity before giving you an answer.

4. Give the individual a written description of what you expect

You know what you want from a volunteer position. However, we often recruit someone and wrongly assume that person knows what we want. It's a recipe for disaster when we don't put our basic expectations for the role in writing. Be as thorough as possible. People appreciate it when they commit to a position and there are no surprises.

5. Give the individual some time to observe and shadow a veteran volunteer

This not only equips your new recruit, but it impresses on your existing volunteers the value of mentor-based training.

6. Provide adequate training

We all know this is important, but very few people do it. Some make the excuse that they don't have time to do the training, but when the new recruit starts making mistakes, you will have to invest more time on the back end to correct what's wrong. Be wise and make the training investment on the front end.

7. Follow up within thirty days to see how the recruit is doing

Within the first thirty to sixty days, your new recruit will surely begin to experience some disappointments, defeats, or disillusionment that could dampen his or her enthusiasm. Your recruit will also have things to celebrate. Following up at the end of thirty days to encourage and coach him or her will mean a happier, more productive team member.

When recruitment is done well, people feel honored and enthusiastic about serving on a successful team. Equally, they will be more effective at helping accomplish the mission of your area of responsibility.

If you've recruited anyone in the past, what was the most critical mistake you made in the recruiting process? What did you learn from it?

Which of the seven steps listed above do you think will be the easiest for you? Why?

Which of the seven steps do you think will be most challenging for you? Why?

What actions can you take to improve in your area of biggest challenge?

As you think of recruiting people to serve on a team, do you feel more nervous or excited? Why?

What action steps do you need to take over the next thirty days to improve your recruiting skills?

Put It Into Practice

Developing a new skill requires practice. Complete the following assignments to help you practice recruiting others.

1. Interview a volunteer who serves in the community or at church and ask what made him or her agree to serve in that role. Write their responses here.

2. Observe your trainer asking a potential team member or leader to join a team. What aspects of this module's insights did your trainer do well? What did your trainer do intentionally? What would you do differently?

3. Make a list of names of people you know who could potentially serve on your team. In what role would you recruit them to serve? What traits do they have that make them a good fit for that role?

Reflect on Your Learning

Where did you grow the most in this competency?

What next step do you need to take to continue to grow in this competency?

Meet with Your Trainer

Consistent practice can be a great beginning to sharpening a skill, but developing skill also requires processing what you learned with others. Meet with your trainer and discuss what you learned from this module.

6

Navigating Conflict

Introduction

If you are leading a group of people, at some point you will experience conflict. Disagreements are inevitable in teams. But conflict doesn't have to be destructive or divisive. God can actually use conflict to produce greater levels of understanding, compassion, grace, and unity. As a leader of leaders, you may not be directly involved with the conflict, but there are times you will be expected to help navigate it. It's like being asked to step in and defuse a bomb! It is a dangerous but important task. We must handle these complex situations in ways that reflect biblical principles of healthy community and that honor those involved.

Deepen Your Character: *Patience*
Leaders must be gentle when navigating conflict and bear with others' shortcomings with the higher goal of developing their spiritual maturity.

Develop Your Competency: Navigating Conflict
Manage conflict in a way that honors God and those involved.

Objectives

1. Assess your ability to practice patience throughout the process of managing conflict, and identify one specific step for growth in this area.

2. Analyze a past conflict to identify the communication styles used.

3. Assess your level of proficiency in following the six steps of navigating conflict.

4. Identify next steps to help you grow in your competency of managing conflict in a way that honors God and those involved.

Deepen Your Character: *Patience*

There are many technical skills involved with navigating conflict, but they must be paired with patience. Galatians 5 says that *patience* is a fruit of the Spirit (ESV). That means it is supernaturally imbued in us when we allow the Holy Spirit to transform our hearts and minds. When those you are trying to lead are argumentative and difficult to work with, it can try your patience. But remember that conflict is often a symptom of spiritual immaturity. What is your patience quota in regards to the spiritual development of those you are leading? Are you disappointed when you don't see much progress right away? Can conflict derail your long-term goals for the group?

Paul likely asked himself similar questions. The church at Ephesus, like many early churches Paul was discipling, had its fair share of conflict. At the heart of the city was a famous temple to the Greek goddess Artemis. Many people converted to Christianity because of Paul's preaching, but many others did not like the impact Christianity had on their previously all-pagan community. One prominent silversmith, Demetrius, saw his business suffer because his customers, who previously bought items used to worship Artemis, were converting to Christianity. Paul knew it would be tough for Christians to grow in this environment, so in his letter to the Ephesians he stressed the gentleness, humility, and forbearance needed to navigate conflict so their faith would grow. When your patience is tested, it reveals your character—and this was of utmost importance to Paul.

Scripture

As you read the following Scripture, meditate on what the author wishes to communicate, and answer the questions below. Allow the Holy Spirit to speak to you and challenge you as a leader in this area so that you deal with conflict effectively and thus continually change the culture of your organization.

Ephesians 4:2–6

Be completely humble and gentle; be patient, bearing with one another in love. Make every effort to keep the unity of the Spirit through the bond of peace. There is one body and one Spirit, just as you were called to one hope when you were called; one Lord, one faith, one baptism; one God and Father of all, who is over all and through all and in all.

As you think about demonstrating patience in the midst of navigating conflict, what part of this passage stands out the most to you? Why?

Think of a time you saw conflict management in a personal, ministry, or business setting handled in an inappropriate or unwise way. How was impatience part of the problem?

What was the outcome?

What are the behaviors unique to you that demonstrate your impatience with others? (For example, raising your voice, talking "down" to others, etc.)

To assess your patience with others, look at the following statements based on Ephesians 4. Think of a recent situation where you tried to navigate conflict among two or more people. Reflect on your attitudes and behavior. Mark each trait red, yellow or green. Red = I am not demonstrating this area. Yellow = I could be more intentional in this area. Green = I am demonstrating this consistently.

I practiced **humility**, listening before I spoke and putting their need to be heard first.

I was **gentle** in the way I spoke, choosing my words and my tone of voice carefully.

I was **patient** when they frustrated me, disagreed with me and/or the mediation process took much longer than anticipated.

I was willing to **bear with** temporary immaturity in order to develop the group spiritually.

Write down one insight this exercise reveals about your character.

Write down one action step you need to take to grow in that area.

Having examined the character trait of patience, we can now begin to work through the core competency for this module: **Manage conflict in a way that honors God and those involved**.

As you read through this section, note how the character trait of patience can undergird a leader's competency in navigating conflict.

Developing Your Competency: *Navigating Conflict*
Pre-Assessment

Before proceeding, complete the assessment below. In the final module of this training guide, you will retake it as a post-assessment to measure your transformation and growth regarding this competency.

The following proficiencies demonstrate mastery of this module's competency.

Grade yourself on each of these proficiencies A, B, C, D or E. Giving yourself an A+ indicates you are a model for others to follow. An E indicates no mastery.

Proficiency	Pre-Assessment
I deal with conflict quickly when it arises.	
I prioritize getting a discussion going when I mediate conflict.	
I am conscious of my tone and emotions and the example I'm setting in the mediation.	
I challenge all parties to practice active listening.	
I am confident and competent to process the issue with follow-up questions after everyone's been heard.	
I ask for help from the supervising pastor when needed.	

Reflection Question

Different people respond to conflict in different ways. What is your instinctive reaction when you find yourself having to navigate conflict? Why?

Navigating Conflict Among Team Members

There are times the leaders you are overseeing will experience conflict with someone on their team or someone in their group. When necessary, your goal is to step in and follow a biblical process that will lead to a restoration of a healthy relationship. But that isn't always easy, and at times it's not even possible because of the responses of those involved.

When conflict arises, people's first inclination is to run, blame, or punch back. And when you are in the middle, attempting to navigate the conflict for others, you too can be tempted to be driven by emotions rather than patience. In order to model handling conflict from a position of truth and grace, you must counteract those emotions.

You must help each person see God's perspective, honor each other's perspectives, and act to preserve the unity of the relationships and the team.

When handled carefully and skilfully, conflict can be good for teams. It can help people understand each other better and develop a closer relationship.

When my children were little, navigating conflict was a common occurrence for me as a father. My two youngest, Jordan and Brianna, were about as close as two siblings could get. But as much as they loved each other, there were times they would still get into arguments. On more than one occasion, I would be sitting in the living room when one of them would run in and start tattling on the other. Two best friends were suddenly at a standoff as enemies. I wanted to help them navigate their conflict, rather than solving it for them, so I would have them sit facing each other and ask each one to explain to the other why they were upset. Inevitably, Jordan would begin to tell Brianna why he was upset, but within a few seconds he would turn to me and say, "And, Dad, she …" At this point I would stop him mid-sentence and explain that his challenge was with his sister, not with me. I redirected his focus and reminded him to talk to her directly. Then I would ask Brianna to share her side. Like her brother she would eventually turn to me, explaining why she was upset.

Each time I stopped them I would coach them on their tone. I would advise them not to use accusatory words and instead practice listening to each other. The more they would talk to each other, the more they understood each other's point of view. If they "apologized" but didn't really mean it, I would call them on their insincerity! Then I'd have them talk it through "until you feel better about this." Then there was that moment of breakthrough, and they would say sorry from a sincere heart. At that point I would encourage them to hug, telling them, "I want you to understand, conflict should always end in an embrace." I wanted them to learn that if you couldn't hug afterward, then there was likely still a hint of resentment built up in the relationship.

I've used the same principles and approach when navigating conflict between spouses, team members, or key leaders in the church. Working to help people drop their guard, seeing the other perspective, and pursuing true reconciliation are applicable principles, whatever our age. People are uncomfortable confronting conflict and often will make concessions or compromises they really don't want to make just to get out of the difficult conversation faster. As a skilled conflict navigator, don't just listen to the words people say, read their posture, their body language, and the "spirit" they are demonstrating as well.

When conflict is handled biblically, it should lead to deeper levels of understanding and intimacy. But for this to happen, it's important that you understand the source of conflict, the dangers of unresolved conflict, the different styles of communication, and the steps to help you navigate the conflict in a biblical manner.

The Source: Why We Experience Conflict

Why do people experience conflict? James spells it out: "What causes fights and quarrels among you? Don't they come from your desires that battle within you?" (James 4:1). The ultimate source of all disagreements is selfishness. We're hardwired to want our own way! Learning to see and accept others' perspectives is a part of the spiritual maturity process. But since not everyone is at the same point on the spiritual journey, we can easily find ourselves at odds with someone who disagrees with us.

While selfishness is the source of conflict, miscommunication and opposing personality types feed that source. Sure, there are times a core problem needs to be worked through. But I have discovered, most of the time, the "issue" really isn't an issue at all. It's a misunderstanding or a personality difference that's causing the trouble. Once communication is clarified or personality quirks are understood, the arguing parties often find they actually agree on the main issue!

Disagreeing parties can have a healthy conversation and work together in a spirit of unity in order to create a positive plan of action that honors God. This will require collaboration, compromise, and maturity from all those involved.

Consequences of Conflict

When conflict is not handled well, there are at least three negative effects:

1. Loss of relationship

Team culture can become toxic if conflict isn't dealt with appropriately. People can become cynical, fearful, and self-protective. Pressure builds up in the team that has to come out somewhere: people begin to express unhelpful opinions on the matter and dishonor the people involved rather than hold their tongues. If not handled correctly and quickly, long-term relational damage can take place. That's why you must respond to conflict with urgency!

2. Loss of respect

When people are defensive or acting in self-protection, they will do and say things that hurt others. Sometimes, in an effort to make themselves look good, they do things to make others look bad. And this type of immature response causes others to lose respect for the individual behaving this way. Once respect is lost, it is hard to regain.

3. Loss of momentum

There is nothing like a disagreement to halt the forward momentum of a group or a team. They can be making great strides toward the vision, when suddenly a disagreement becomes a distraction and progress comes to a halt. Instead of giving attention and effort to the vision, the focus is now on the problem.

Think back to previous conflicts you've encountered. What seemed to be the root cause of the conflict? (When sharing in your training session, do not reveal names, sensitive information, or give information that would disclose who was involved in the conflict.)

What did you learn about navigating conflict from those experiences?

Think of a time when a conflict you were either a part of or were aware of ended with true, healthy reconciliation. What factors helped achieve reconciliation?

Understanding Communication Styles

As we saw in the Deepen Your Character section, Paul gives a set of guiding principles for how we should behave in the midst of conflict. He continues in Ephesians 4:

> Get rid of all bitterness, rage and anger, brawling and slander, along with every form of malice. Be kind and compassionate to one another, forgiving each other, just as in Christ God forgave you.
>
> Ephesians 4:31–32

Unfortunately, not everyone responds with that level of spiritual maturity. Every person tends to have a default conflict management mode, and these are summarized in four different communication styles. Understanding these four styles will help you grasp why someone is reacting the way they are and help you adapt your approach in course-correcting the situation.

Communication Style 1—Passive

Those who use this style tend to be uncomfortable with conflict and confrontation. For this reason, they will try to avoid conflict by suppressing their feelings. They may be hesitant or even fearful of speaking up and sharing their opinion. Often they believe their feelings aren't being taken into consideration or assume they're being taken advantage of. Resentment is building, even though they remain quiet in a conflict situation. They may even find it difficult to make eye contact.

Communication Style 2—Aggressive

The aggressive style is the opposite of passive. Those who use it are very verbal and confrontational. They do not hesitate to speak their mind and often do so in a way that feels like an attack. They can communicate in ways that hurt and intimidate the other person. They may struggle with listening because they are more concerned with expressing their view and getting their way.

Communication Style 3—Passive-Aggressive

The passive-aggressive communicator is tricky because they appear passive on the surface, but in fact they are acting out of anger. They are very subtle but you can recognize their conflict management strategies: sarcasm, denying that there is a problem, trying to sabotage the reconciliation process, blaming others, or procrastinating in order to "send a message."

Communication Style 4—Assertive

The assertive style is used by someone who truly wants to seek reconciliation. They honestly acknowledge the problem and express a desire to collaborate for a solution. They are honest about their feelings but in a way that honors the other person. They work hard to not have an accusatory tone. They speak respectfully and are willing to compromise in the process of navigating the conflict. This person seeks to understand, not just be understood.

Which communication styles have you seen evidenced in your current group or team you're leading? How has that diversity of styles affected team culture?

Seizing the Opportunity

It may sound contradictory, but conflict is always an opportunity for growth. However, some leaders are so afraid of conflict that they try to defuse it without using it to the team's advantage. Conflict always comes with strong opinions and strong emotions. That's why handling it can be intimidating and uncomfortable. When you're in a room and people are expressing strong, differing opinions, emotions can escalate and cause damage. Don't let emotions get out of control. But also remember that your single goal is *not* to defuse the conflict;

it's to use the conflict to deepen understanding and intimacy among those involved. Defusing it without truly getting to a place of mutual understanding doesn't promote growth. I admit it's not something I ever look forward to, but when conflict arises, I've discovered that my approach determines how the process plays out. Let's look at the steps of a positive approach to conflict below.

Steps for Positively Navigating Conflict

Let me make a disclaimer: if you are serving as a volunteer leader, it would be wise to consult with the pastoral staff leader you report to and alert them to any situation of conflict you are dealing with, so they can coach you through it if necessary. But remember, they have entrusted and empowered you in this role. Prayerfully following the steps below can help you navigate the conflict from the time you schedule a meeting to begin to deal with the conflict, until the time the problem is resolved.

1. Choose to deal with conflict quickly

When you are alerted to the conflict, work hard to get people together for a meeting as quickly as possible. Paul advises us, "'In your anger do not sin': Do not let the sun go down while you are still angry" (Ephesians 4:26). The longer we allow conflict to go unaddressed, the greater the chance things will become distorted and escalate out of control. Remember, there is more than just the relationship of these individuals at stake. Disunity in the body can affect the broader church and at times even have consequences that impact its mission.

Be careful not to engage in one-party conversations. It can be tempting to just talk to one party and get their perspective. This could cause you to have a bias as you attempt to navigate the conflict. Work hard to get both parties together for an open, honest discussion.

2. Get a discussion going

Avoiding a situation makes it worse rather than better. When one of your leaders is struggling with conflict and has asked you to get involved, get the parties together to talk to each other. James warns us, "Know this, my beloved brothers: let every person be quick to hear, slow to speak, slow to anger" (James 1:19 ESV). Your objective is to get the discussion going and help the individuals understand each other's perspective.

My two boys got into a major disagreement as young teens. When I had listened to both of them describe the problem, I realized that the primary issue was they had a different perspective on the situation. So I took a coin that was black on one side and white on the other and held it between my thumb and index finger so each could only see one side of the coin. I asked them what color the coin was. Jordan answered, "White." Brandon answered, "Black." I turned the coin around and said, "You are both right. You just have different perspectives." Then I explained to them that this was the case with their conflict—neither one was right or wrong; they just had a different perspective on the situation. Once they understood the other's perspective, they were much more gracious about the situation. Your job as a leader is similarly to help each person see the other perspective. Often the source of disagreement is a matter of perspective or preference rather than right versus wrong.

3. Set the tone for the group

While those who are at odds with each other may get heated during the discussion, you ultimately set the tone and direction by establishing upfront a clear outcome for the situation and clear guidelines for your time together:

i. Clarify that reconciliation and unity is the objective

I once met with some parents who were very angry at our youth pastor for a programming decision he made that affected their teens. Things had escalated intensely by the time I got involved and they were ready to go to war when we finally met. As I opened that time of discussion, I knew it was critical for me to maintain a calm tone. Solomon points out in Proverbs 15:1, "A gentle answer turns away wrath, but a harsh word stirs up anger." I explained upfront that although they might not feel like it right at that point, a few days ago, they all loved each other and got along. I shared that I believed everyone had been hurt in this circumstance and said, "If we all are patient and honest, we can work toward understanding each other and walk out unified once more."

ii. Pray

Praying together in the meeting invites the Holy Spirit to guide each of you through the process. It's sad, but, prior to your meeting, neither of the parties may have even prayed about the conflict, inviting God to bring resolution. Most of the time disagreeing parties are more concerned about protecting themselves than praying for reconciliation.

iii. Watch your own tone

If you are not careful, your own emotions can get swept up in the conversation and you can unintentionally display frustration, anger or irritation. It's essential, as you engage the parties in conflict, that you manage your own reactions. See yourself as a thermostat that helps set the environment.

iv. Give simple ground rules

You can establish your own ground rules for the meeting, but here are some rules I've found helpful:

- We are going to focus on the facts.
- We are going to be honest about our feelings.
- We are going to seek to understand each other.
- We are going to act in love toward one another.
- We are going to give our very best effort to reconcile.
- We will keep the discussion only among those who are a part of the solution and not talk about this outside to others who are not a part of the solution.

Stating these rules upfront will help better ensure (but not guarantee) people act in a mature manner.

4. Ask each person to listen to the other

Remember that the best way to resolve conflict is through effective communication. Sit down with both parties. Ask them to share their perspective with each other, and challenge them to listen carefully. Choose one person to go first and share the facts from their perspective, as well as what they are feeling. Remind them of Paul's words to the Ephesians:

> Instead, speaking the truth in love, we will grow to become in every respect the mature body of him who is the head, that is, Christ. From him the whole body, joined and held together by every supporting ligament, grows and builds itself up in love, as each part does its work.
> Ephesians 4:15–16

Ask them to commit to being a truth teller, rather than suppressing their thoughts or aggressively attacking the other person.

5. Work toward resolution and reconciliation

After both parties have shared their perspectives, you can begin to ask questions and work toward resolution and reconciliation. Once you've heard both sides, you will be able to spot their differences. Be careful at this point not to minimize anyone's feelings. Remember, as far as they are concerned, their perspective is their reality. The following are a few techniques you can use to process what they just heard and help bring about unity:

- Ask each to restate what they heard the other party say. This will help you to see if they were really listening and understanding.
- Ask clarifying questions. Use your curiosity and empathy to ask questions that could lead to greater understanding.
- Ask for solutions and see what they come up with together.
- When you seem to be making no progress and people are getting frustrated, stop and pray.

6. Elicit help from a more senior leader

There are times the parties involved may make it difficult to resolve the issue, despite your best efforts. If you feel the issue is escalating, and sin is not being confessed or recognized, then it is wise to go to the leader you report to and engage them in the process. Jesus gives us this counsel:

> "If your brother or sister sins, go and point out their fault, just between the two of you. If they listen to you, you have won them over. But if they will not listen, take one or two others along, so that 'every matter may be established by the testimony of two or three witnesses.' If they still refuse to listen, tell it to the church; and if they refuse to listen even to the

church, treat them as you would a pagan or a tax collector."
Matthew 18:15–17

By getting a more senior leader involved, you are simply following the steps Jesus prescribed to help bring unity and reconciliation to the situation.

You may not be entirely comfortable dealing with conflict, but as a leader of leaders you play a critical role in bringing greater levels of unity to the group.

What are some common mistakes leaders make when navigating conflict?

Consider a conflict you've experienced in the past. What mistakes did you make? What communication styles did the people involved use? Reflect and write out how you would navigate that issue more effectively if you were armed with the information you've learned in this module.

Which of the six steps for managing conflict have you mastered?
List below. How have you demonstrated your mastery of these
steps in the past?

Which of the six steps are your weakest? List below. Name one
positive outcome that would result from your growth in this area.

Put It Into Practice

Developing a new skill requires practice. Complete the following assignment to help you practice navigating conflict.

Before meeting with your trainer, ask a close friend or family member to give you honest feedback on how you typically handle conflict. Reference a specific situation if possible. Ask: "How do you think I normally respond to conflict? In what way do I handle it well? What could I do better? How do I come across when I am frustrated? What advice would you give me to better handle conflict as a leader?"

Reflect on Your Learning

Where did you grow the most in this competency?

What next step do you need to take to continue to grow in this competency?

Meet with Your Trainer

Consistent practice can be a great beginning to sharpening a skill, but developing skill also requires processing what you learned with others. Meet with your trainer and discuss what you learned from this module.

7

Review Your Progress

Congratulations! Over the past few weeks and months you have worked your way through six leadership modules, met with your trainer to debrief and discover new insights, and grown in your leadership character and competencies.

During this training, you have had a trainer walk alongside you serving as a model, providing feedback on your leadership, and giving you insights to grow in your character and competency. While it may feel like this journey is over, it is really just beginning.

Leadership is a lifelong learning process. And a big part of that process is doing periodic self-evaluation to discover your strengths as well as the areas in which you need to continue to grow.

In this training guide, each module started by having you self-assess an aspect of your character. Also in each module you did a self-assessment scoring yourself A–E on five proficiencies of each leadership competency. Altogether you evaluated your leadership on thirty proficiencies!

The final step of this training is a post-assessment. You can do this on your own or with your trainer. This is a tool that you can come back to again and again as you continue to grow in your ability to lead leaders.

Post-Assessment: *Character*

This is the step where you must ask yourself, "Where do I want continued growth in this aspect of my *character*?" Now that you have interacted with the content, it is time to reflect on what you have learned. Answer the following character questions and share your reflections during your meeting time with your trainer.

Module 1: Courage

Leaders take bold steps of faith in the face of obstacles and opposition.

What was the biggest thing you learned about this aspect
of your character?

In what way have you seen growth in this area?

What next step do you need to take to continue growing in this aspect of your character?

Module 2: *Integrity*

Leaders are honest and demonstrate consistent character.

What was the biggest thing you learned about this aspect of your character?

In what way have you seen growth in this area?

What next step do you need to take to continue growing in this aspect of your character?

Module 3: *Encouragement*

Leaders encourage others in such a way that it shapes their soul.

What was the biggest thing you learned about this aspect of your character?

In what way have you seen growth in this area?

What next step do you need to take to continue growing in this aspect of your character?

Module 4: *Humility*

Leaders consider the needs of others above their own.

What was the biggest thing you learned about this aspect of your character?

In what way have you seen growth in this area?

What next step do you need to take to continue growing in this aspect of your character?

Module 5: *Passion*

Leaders are filled with a fervent drive toward the cause God has given them.

What was the biggest thing you learned about this aspect of your character?

In what way have you seen growth in this area?

What next step do you need to take to continue growing in this aspect of your character?

Module 6: *Patience*

Leaders must be gentle when navigating conflict and bear with others' shortcomings with the higher goal of developing their spiritual maturity.

What was the biggest thing you learned about this aspect of your character?

In what way have you seen growth in this area?

What next step do you need to take to continue growing in this aspect of your character?

Post-Assessment: Competency

This is the step where you must ask yourself, "Where do I want continued growth in my *competencies*?" Now that you have interacted with the content and put it into practice, it is time to reflect on what you have learned.

Add in your pre-assessment results to the following tables and then score yourself again, based on the degree of growth you feel you've experienced (for example you might have scored yourself a pre-assessment C, post-assessment B). Giving yourself an A+ indicates you are a model for others to follow. An E indicates no mastery. Then answer the questions and share your reflections during your meeting time with your trainer.

Module 1: *Spiritual Leadership*

Develop the heart and practices of a spiritual leader so you can leave a legacy for others to emulate.

Proficiency	Pre-Assessment	Post-Assessment	Notes
I am constantly making efforts to grow spiritually.			
I regularly connect relationally with those I am leading.			
I consistently challenge those I am leading.			
I practice active listening.			
I prioritize praying for my leaders.			

Where did I grow the most in this competency?

What next step do I need to take to continue to grow in this competency?

Module 2: *Values-Based Leadership*

Embody your values and lead in a way to create practices and patterns that reflect those values and move the team toward the common goal and vision.

Proficiency	Pre-Assessment	Post-Assessment	Notes
My team has clearly defined values.			
I share these values with the people I'm leading early and often.			
I approach decision-making through the grid of my values.			
I model my church's core values consistently.			
I utilize a process for systematically evaluating our values.			

Proficiency	Pre-Assessment	Post-Assessment	Notes
I do not allow challenging circumstances to alter our values.			
I am careful to celebrate successful implementation of our core values.			

Where did I grow the most in this competency?

What next step do I need to take to continue to grow in this competency?

Module 3: *Bringing out the Best in Others*

Learn how to bring out the best in others through encouraging and challenging them toward maximizing their strengths.

Proficiency	Pre-Assessment	Post-Assessment	Notes
The encourage-ment I give is sincere.			
The encourage-ment I give is specific.			
The encourage-ment I give is strengths-focused.			
I regularly and intentionally try to catch people doing things right.			
I know my leaders' strengths.			
I encourage their strengths.			
I challenge them toward growth.			

Where did I grow the most in this competency?

What next step do I need to take to continue to grow in this competency?

Module 4: *Leading Huddles*

Lead a huddle in a way that unites, develops, and challenges members to more effectively lead their team/group.

Proficiency	Pre-Assessment	Post-Assessment	Notes
I regularly ask follow-up questions.			
I lead a huddle with high intentionality and accomplish intended objectives.			
I create a sense of community among a group of leaders.			
I facilitate discussion that leads to discovery.			
I encourage and challenge leaders in the context of the huddle meeting.			

Where did I grow the most in this competency?

What next step do I need to take to continue to grow in this competency?

Module 5: Recruiting Leaders

Expand your team by following a deliberate recruitment process.

Proficiency	Pre-Assessment	Post-Assessment	Notes
I give potential recruits time to pray about the decision.			
I tell the individual why I chose him or her.			
I ensure his or her gifts and passions fit the position.			
I provide a written description of expectations.			
I make sure he or she observes and shadows a veteran volunteer.			
I provide adequate training for the position.			
I follow up within thirty days after recruiting a new person.			

Where did I grow the most in this competency?

What next step do I need to take to continue to grow in this competency?

Module 6: *Navigating Conflict*

Manage conflict in a way that honors God and those involved.

Proficiency	Pre-Assessment	Post-Assessment	Notes
I deal with conflict quickly when it arises.			
I prioritize getting a discussion going when I mediate conflict.			
I am conscious of my tone and emotions and the example I'm setting in the mediation.			
I challenge all parties to practice active listening.			
I am confident and competent to process the issue with follow-up questions after everyone's been heard.			
I ask for help from the supervising pastor when needed.			

Where did I grow the most in this competency?

What next step do I need to take to continue to grow in this competency?

Huddle Samples

Long Huddle Sample

Huddle Topic: How to Remain Relevant

 ### Connect

What is your favorite coffee shop in town and why?

 ### Celebrate

What has been a win in your area of ministry you've noticed in the past month?

 ### Coach

Competency: Understand your culture and adapt to it in order to remain relevant.

Discussion Question: What's your favorite innovation over the past ten years?

1 Corinthians 9:19–23

Though I am free and belong to no one, I have made myself a slave to everyone, to win as many as possible. To the Jews I became like a Jew, to win the Jews. To those under the law I became like one under the law (though I myself am not under the law), so as to win those under the law. To those not having the law I became like one not having the law (though I am not free from God's law but am under Christ's law), so as to win those not having the law. To the weak I became weak, to win the weak. I have become all things to all people so that by all possible means I might save some. I do all this for the sake of the gospel, that I may share in its blessings.

What phrase stood out to you from this passage? Why?

Paul lists different types of people he seeks to reach: Jews, those under the law, those not having the law, the weak. How would you describe the different types of people in your target community?

What are the unique perspectives or distinctives of these groups regarding Christ?

What adjustments do you feel you need to make to better understand and connect with those you're trying to reach?

Rick Warren Ted Talk: How to Stay Relevant
https://www.youtube.com/watch?v=LFdRFhVQwvU

D_____

N _____

A _____

Discussion Questions

What challenged your thinking the most?

What questions did this video raise for you?

What leadership strength did it affirm in you?

What growth area did it reveal for you?

What ideas did it stir for you?

What are 2–3 action steps you need to take?

Communicate

(Write below information your team needs to be aware of.)

_____

_____

_____

_____

_____

_____

 **Care**

How can we pray for each other today?

Short Huddle Sample

Huddle Topic: Providing Excellent Customer Service

Every church and every organization is ultimately aimed at serving people. While "customer" may not be a great term for those who attend our church, we certainly want to make sure we are serving those who attend with the very best we have.

In this huddle you will facilitate a discussion on how you and your team can provide memorable experiences that help people realize they are valued in the eyes of God and in the eyes of the church.

 **Connect**

If you're leading a short huddle, you can just do a quick welcome, skip the "Connect" piece, and go straight to: "Celebrate." (This is to maximize time as a short huddle is completed in about twelve to fifteen minutes.)

 Celebrate (2 minutes)

What has been a win in your area of ministry you've noticed in the past month?

 Coach (8–10 minutes)

What has been the best customer service experience you've ever had?

Let's watch this short video from Bill Capodagli, the author of *The Disney Way*, where he talks about excellent customer service. After watching, we will talk through some of our takeaways. https://www.youtube.com/watch?v=DlR5gcxyL_s

■ What stood out to you the most from the video?

■ What is a scriptural example of serving others with excellence?

■ What are two to three ways we could provide better "customer service" in our area of ministry?

■ What is one way we can apply what we learned right away?

Takeaway to share: When you serve others with excellence, God is using you to express how much he values them.

🎤 Communicate (2 minutes)

(Write below information your team needs to be aware of.)

_____

_____

_____

_____

_____

 **Care (2 minutes)**

How can we pray for each other today?

Trainer Guide

As a leader of leaders, you have much wisdom and insight to offer those who are in the process of moving to this level of leadership. The Leading Leaders training is designed to help these individuals gain the knowledge and experience needed to effectively lead at this new level.

All the questions from the modules have been organized in a simple way below so you can seamlessly flow through the training questions to help those you are training learn from what they've read and put into practice.

The following tips will help you as you lead an individual or a small cohort through the training modules.

Tips

Schedule
Before meeting with your trainees, create a proposed schedule of when and where you will meet. A fortnightly rhythm will give them plenty of time to read the module and do the assignments. However, do not try to rush the process. If your trainees are struggling to grasp one of the modules, slow down to ensure they get what they need to grow in that area of character or competency.

Model
Modeling is one of the most effective means of training others. Invite the trainee to observe you in your leadership role so that you can

model these particular competencies. For example, if you are leading a huddle with your leaders, ask your trainees to come and observe. After they have observed you, ask them what they learned from watching you in action.

Assign

While each module gives them "Put It Into Practice" assignments, feel free to change those to give them assignments that fit the particular ministry role they are being trained for.

Meet

When you meet with those you are training, I recommend you schedule fifty to seventy-five minutes. Each module has more content than you can cover in that amount of time, so preview the questions and mark those that will bring out the most learning. Don't feel like you have to cover every single question. A typical fifty to seventy-five-minute training session will look something like this:

 ## Connect (5–10 minutes)

Spend the first few minutes allowing the group to connect relationally, catch up on what's been going on in their week. Avoid just rushing into the content. Remember you want this to be a relational approach to development, which means allowing people time to get to know each other well.

 ## Celebrate (5 minutes)

Ask, "What is something we've seen God do since the last time we met that we can celebrate?" You don't have to spend a lot of time on this, but take a few minutes and enjoy the work God is doing in their lives or in their ministries. This celebration time can reveal some important things in the lives of these leaders and can deepen their faith as they watch how God is working in each other's lives.

 ## Coach (30–45 minutes)

Walk through all the questions and assessments. The trainee should have worked through all the content of the module before you meet with them, so you are asking them to discuss issues they have already considered and reflected on personally. The material provided is more than enough for a forty-five-minute discussion. Make sure you are prepared to discuss what is most relevant for your particular learners. Also, you may choose to spend more than one meeting to cover one module.

 ## Communicate (1–2 minutes)

Ask, "What important upcoming events do we all need to be aware of?" You won't need to spend much more than one minute on this. But it is important to communicate any key events coming up at the church as well as the details for your next training session.

 ## Care (10–15 minutes)

Make sure you save time to ask, "How can we pray for each other?" Spend a few minutes praying with and for each other.

While this is a general guide, remember to be flexible and allow the Holy Spirit to use you to help each learner truly grasp and learn what God has for them in each module.

Facilitate

Remember, as a trainer, you are a facilitator of discussion. It is important to get your trainees talking about what they learned. The temptation will be to talk too much and tell them everything you know about each of the topics. While your experience and insights are important, it is just as important that your learners verbalize what they are learning. Utilize the questions to guide them to share what they are discovering, then share your insights as a supplement to their learning experience. I always tell my trainers, "The questions in the modules stimulate thought and provide good answers, but your follow-up questions are where your learners will find the gold." I recommend using the Five Hats (see pages 120–121) to stimulate a deeper level of thinking.

Module Questions

Module 1: *Practicing Spiritual Leadership*

In this module we will focus on deepening your courage and developing your competency of spiritual leadership.

 ### Deepen Your *Character: Courage*

Let's begin by focusing on the character portion of this study. In this module the focus is on: **Courage**—*Leaders take bold steps of faith in the face of obstacles and opposition.*

Read Acts 20:17–27 together.

Acts 20:17–27

From Miletus, Paul sent to Ephesus for the elders of the church. When they arrived, he said to them: "You know how I lived the whole time I was with you, from the first day I came into the province of Asia. I served the Lord with great humility and with tears and in the midst of severe testing by the plots of my Jewish opponents. You know that I have not hesitated to preach anything that would be helpful to you but have taught you publicly and from house to house. I have declared to both Jews and Greeks that they must turn to God in repentance and have faith in our Lord Jesus.

"And now, compelled by the Spirit, I am going to Jerusalem, not knowing what will happen to me there. I only know that in every city the Holy Spirit warns me that prison and hardships are facing me. However, I consider my life worth nothing to me; my only aim is to finish the race and complete the task the Lord Jesus has given me—the task of testifying to the good news of God's grace.

"Now I know that none of you among whom I have gone about preaching the kingdom will ever see me again. Therefore, I declare to you today that I am innocent of the blood of any of you. For I have not hesitated to proclaim to you the whole will of God."

■ Share about a time you saw courageous leadership in action. How did that courageous act impact you personally?

■ This passage is laced with evidence that Paul was a courageous leader. List the words or phrases in this passage where you see examples of his leadership courage.

■ To assess the measure of your character, let's look at how well you consistently demonstrate courage as a spiritual leader. To begin, make a list of at least three traits of a courageous leader that you see demonstrated in this passage. Write them below and mark each trait red, yellow or green. Red = I am not demonstrating this area. Yellow = I could be more intentional in this area. Green = I am demonstrating this consistently.

- Write down one insight this exercise reveals about your character.

- Write down one action step you need to take to grow in your courage.

 Develop Your Competency:
Spiritual Leadership

Now that we've talked about how we can grow in courage, let's talk through what you learned about the competency: **Spiritual Leadership**—*Develop the heart and practices of a spiritual leader so you can leave a legacy for others to emulate.*

- Who do you think is the most admired spiritual leader in America today? Why?

Demonstrating Spiritual Leadership

- Reflect on some of the people you have been led by. What did you most admire about their character?

- What leadership skill did they consistently demonstrate that made them such a good leader?

■ What would you most like to emulate from the way they lead?

Two Keys to Becoming a Leader Worth Following

■ Make a list of leadership spirit characteristics and leadership skill requirements. Evaluate yourself against both lists and identify ways to make progress at your weakest points.

Leadership Spirit	Leadership Skill

■ What did this list reveal to you about areas you could grow in?

Five Traits of a Spiritual Leader

■ When you are leading leaders you have to think and lead differently than when you are leading team members. What do you think the leaders you are, or will be, leading want most from you?

Scenario: *Sue was just trained to be a new coach (leader of leaders) in her church. While she was excited about the opportunity to influence the five leaders who were now placed under her care, she was met with a less than enthusiastic response. Knowing the importance of building relationships with these leaders, she started out by making one-on-one contact with each one, inviting them to grab coffee over the next few weeks. But only one of four confirmed a date and time to do so. The others indicated they were busy and would get back to her. She has now been in the role for three months and finds herself very discouraged. While she does communicate with these leaders through email and occasional calls, it just seems they aren't responsive to making a connection with her and allowing her to provide the encouragement and coaching she would like to give.*

- What could be potential reasons Sue is getting this non-enthusiastic response?

- What would you do in her situation? Why?

- What challenges do you anticipate in getting others to readily respond to your leadership?

- Reflect back on the five traits of a spiritual leader. Which one do you feel is your greatest strength?

- Which one will be your greatest challenge? Why?

- What can you do to grow in this area of greatest challenge?

Developing Character in Your Leaders

- If you were teaching a young leader how to shape the character of the individuals on his or her team, what advice would you give them?

Put It Into Practice

Developing a new skill requires practice. Discuss with those you are training what they learned about spiritual leadership from their "Put It Into Practice" assignments.

The assignments were to:

1. Try using the 5-P agenda for a one-on-one with a friend, family member or someone on your team.

- What did you do well?

- What could you do better?

- How comfortable were you leading this type of conversation? How comfortable was the other person?

2. Think of a situation you're facing right now requiring leadership courage, and work that situation through the grid of four questions to process your options and come to a conclusion that you will act on.

i. What options do you have?

ii. What are the consequences of each option?

iii. What is the wise thing to do?

iv. What's the price you will have to pay for making the right decision?

Reflect on Your Learning

- Where did you grow the most in this competency?

- What next step do you need to take to continue to grow in this competency?

Module 2: Practicing Values-Based Leadership

In this module we will focus on deepening your integrity and developing your competency of practicing values-based leadership.

 Deepen Your Character: *Integrity*

Let's begin by focusing on the character portion of this study. In this module the focus is on: **Integrity**—*Leaders are honest and demonstrate consistent character.*

Read Proverbs 4:25–27 together.

Proverbs 4:25–27

Let your eyes look straight
ahead;
fix your gaze directly before you.
Give careful thought to the
paths for your feet
and be steadfast in all your
ways.
Do not turn to the right or the left;
keep your foot from evil.

■ Which of the three pressures can most likely cause you personally to not act with integrity: the desire to please people; the need to impress people; or the urge to protect self?

■ Which phrase from this passage do you most need to focus on in order to help you lead with greater levels of integrity? Why?

■ Living with integrity means talking and acting in ways that are consistent with godly character. Defining and acting on our personal values can help us act with greater levels of integrity. Write out three core values you, as a leader, try to embody in your walk with Christ.

■ Now put a grade beside each value, based on how well you think you are embodying each one.

■ Which value do you live out most consistently? How is that value demonstrated in your actions?

■ Which value do you want to improve on? What are some ways that value could be better demonstrated in your actions?

■ What did this exercise reveal about your integrity?

■ What action step do you need to take to grow in your integrity?

 ## Develop Your Competency: *Values-Based Leadership*

Now that we've talked about how we can grow in integrity, let's talk through what you learned about the competency: **Values-Based Leadership**—*Embody your values and lead in a way to create practices and patterns that reflect those values and move the team toward the common goal and vision.*

■ Describe a business, organization, or church you've encountered whose values are very evident. What specific behaviors did you observe that made their values so evident?

Are Your Values Adding Value?

■ Imagine you were asked to teach a group of young leaders about the importance of values-based leadership. Write out three to five key points you would share with them. What illustration could you use to make your point?

Traits of a Values-Driven Leader

■ Who is the best values-based leader you know? What would you like to emulate about their leadership in order to become a better value-based leader?

■ List each of the values of your church below. (If there are no defined values, list what seem to be the top three values, based on your experience.)

■ Next, write "demonstrated by" statements for each describing how you can live out those values in your leadership role. Now find ways to intentionally live out one of those values at home, work, and church over the next week.

■ Which of the seven traits in this section are you best at executing?

■ Which of the seven traits do you need to grow in the most? What are some ways you can do so?

- Think of someone you are currently leading. How can you encourage them to better demonstrate one of the values of your church or team?

Put It Into Practice

Developing a new skill requires practice. Discuss with those you are training what they learned about values-based leadership from their "Put It Into Practice" assignment.

The assignment was to:

Write down a key decision you have to make at work, home, or in ministry and filter the decision through the core values of that particular environment. Then record how the values impacted the decision you made and how you handled the situation. Share what you did and what you learned from this experience.

Reflect on Your Learning

- Where did you grow the most in this competency?

- What next step do you need to take to continue to grow in this competency?

Module 3: Bringing out the Best in Your Leaders

In this module we will focus on deepening your spirit of encouragement and developing your competency of bringing out the best in others.

Deepen Your Character: *Encouragement*

Let's begin by focusing on the character portion of this study. In this module the focus is on: **Encouragement**—*Leaders encourage others in such a way that it shapes their soul.*

Read Hebrews 3:12–13 together.

Hebrews 3:12–13

See to it, brothers and sisters, that none of you has a sinful, unbelieving heart that turns away from the living God. But encourage one another daily, as long as it is called "Today," so that none of you may be hardened by sin's deceitfulness.

- Who has been the biggest encourager in your life? In what ways has that person encouraged you?

- What one word in Hebrews 3:12–13 stands out to you the most? Why?

- Why do you think God repeatedly tells us in his Word to "encourage one another?"

- On a scale of 1 to 5, how would you rate yourself as an encourager?

(1= I am not a good encourager at all; 2 = I try but I know I'm not good at it; 3 = I tell people I appreciate them, but don't think I am a great encourager; 4 = I am consistent in encouraging others but have room to grow; 5= I am a model others can learn from and emulate.)

■ Why did you give yourself that score?

■ What one thing could you do to become a better encourager?

 ## Develop Your Competency: *Bring Out the Best In Others*

Now that we've talked about how we can grow as an encourager, let's talk through what you learned about the competency: **Bring Out the Best In Others**—*Learn how to bring out the best in others through encouraging and challenging them toward maximizing their strengths.*

■ What would you say is your greatest strength?

■ How did you come to discover this?

Strengths of Your Leaders

■ Make a list of those who currently serve under your leadership, either at work or at church. Beside each name, write out what you believe to be their top strength. To what degree do you feel they are maximizing their strength?

■ Whose strengths do you need to get to know better?

■ What specific things will you do to help you better understand their strengths?

- Looking again at the names of those who you lead, choose one or two people. How could you help them better maximize their strengths.

Encourage Their Strengths

- Which of the three traits are you best at when you encourage someone: Sincerity, Specificity, or Strengths-focused?

- Which of these three traits do you need to grow in the most?

- Think of leaders in your area of ministry. What are some common discouragements they tend to face in their leadership role? Make a list below.

- As you discovered in answering the previous question, leaders can face a variety of factors that lead to discouragement. And discouragement can cause a leader to stop leading and miss out on the impact God is calling them to make by using their gifts.

Imagine one of your leaders comes to you and informs you she is about to "take a break" from leading for a while. She has been leading in this particular area of ministry for a little over a year and you felt she was doing a good job in her role. When you dig into why she wants to take a break, you get a sense she is not so much tired as she is discouraged. Obviously, if God is calling her to take a break, then you mustn't stand in her way. But if a spirit of discouragement, rather than the Holy Spirit, is influencing her decision, then God can use you to help her persevere.

- Considering what you learned in the first module about being a spiritual leader and what you've learned so far in this module about bringing out the best in others, what would you do to help this leader further process her decision to take a break?

Challenge Them to Grow Their Strengths

■ Consider the Invitation–Challenge matrix. Which are you better at: Invitation or Challenge?

■ Looking at the names of those you lead, what does each person need the most from you right now: Invitation or Challenge? Write an "I" or a "C" for Invitation or Challenge respectively next to their name in the table.

Put It Into Practice

Developing a new skill requires practice. Discuss with those you are training what they learned about bringing out the best in their leaders from their "Put It Into Practice" assignments.

The assignments were to:

1. Practice giving encouragement to at least three people. Encourage a family member, co-worker, someone on your ministry team, and/ or a friend using the principles you learned in this module. Take note of how each person responds and reflect on these questions:

■ What did you do well?

■ What could you do better?

■ How comfortable were you giving the encouragement?

2. Choose someone from your team and lead them through a strengths conversation to help them be more aware of their strengths and how they use them.

■ Who did you choose? Why?

■ How did you structure that discussion with them?

■ What did you learn about helping people play to their strengths from this exercise?

Reflect on Your Learning

■ Where did you grow the most in this competency?

■ What next step do you need to take to continue to grow in this competency?

Module 4: Leading Huddles

In this module we will focus on deepening your humility and developing your competency of leading huddles.

 Deepen Your Character: *Humility*

Let's begin by focusing on the character portion of this study. In this module the focus is on: **Humility**—*Leaders consider the needs of others above their own.*

Read Philippians 2:5–8 together.

Philippians 2:5–8

In your relationships with one another, have the same mindset as Christ Jesus:
Who, being in very nature God,
    did not consider equality with God
        something to be used to his own
        advantage;
rather, he made himself nothing
    by taking the very nature of a servant,
    being made in human likeness.
And being found in appearance as a man,
    he humbled himself
    by becoming obedient to death—
        even death on a cross!

- Think of a leader you know whose humility attracts others to follow him or her? What do you learn from their example?

- What part of your personality makes it sometimes difficult for you to demonstrate humility?

- Paul tells us Jesus took on the nature of a servant. Thinking back to the Gospels, when was a time you recall Jesus demonstrating servant leadership? What impact did that action have in the moment?

- Take some time to evaluate how well you are developing in the area of humility. Admittedly, our levels of humility and pride are easier for others to see in us than for us to see in ourselves. You may therefore find it helpful to invite a close friend to do this exercise with you and ask for their input.

Remember, humility is a situational character quality for most people. It's easier to be humble in certain circumstances and more difficult in others. Using the following "Humility Meter," rate yourself in the following situations by placing a mark on the line between pride and humility to represent your current attitude:

At work
Pride - - -- - - - - - - - - - - Humility
At home with family
Pride - - -- - - - - - - - - - - Humility
Among friends you know really well
Pride - - -- - - - - - - - - - - Humility
Among peers you don't really know well
Pride - - -- - - - - - - - - - - Humility
When executing a leadership role
Pride - - -- - - - - - - - - - - Humility

- In what area do you most consistently demonstrate humility? Why do you think this is the case?

- Looking at some of the lower scores, write down one way you can practice humility this week.

Develop Your Competency: Leading Huddles

Now that we've talked about how we can grow in humility, let's talk through what you learned about the competency: **Leading Huddles**—*Lead a huddle in a way that unites, develops, and challenges members to more effectively lead their team/group.*

- What is your favorite and least favorite part of meetings?

How to Lead a Huddle

- How would you describe your confidence level on a scale of 1–5 in leading a huddle as described in this module: 1 – I am not confident, 3 – I am somewhat confident, 5 – I am highly confident? If you scored 1 or 2, what is your biggest concern in leading huddles? If you scored 3, what area do you need to grow in the most to increase your confidence level? If you scored 4 or 5, what strength do you bring to leading huddles?

- What common mistakes do you think huddle leaders make? Which of those do you fear you will be guilty of making?

Huddle Nuts and Bolts

- Write down some of the topics you think the leaders in your area of ministry would want to grow in (e.g., soul care, delegating responsibility, handling difficult people, etc.).

- Imagine you have been leading huddles every other month for eight months now. One of your leaders has not shown interest in the huddles and has only attended one out of the four you've led. What excuses might that leader give for not attending?

- How would you counteract those excuses?

- What would you do to encourage this leader to engage in these regular huddles?

Ask effective follow-up questions

- Which of the five types of follow-up question do you use most often or most naturally in conversation with others (Fisherman, Reporter, Physician, Contractor, Pilot)?

- Which one(s) will you try to implement more often as a result of reading this module? Explain.

Put It Into Practice

Developing a new skill requires practice. Discuss with those you are training what they learned about leading huddles from their "Put It Into Practice" assignments.

The assignments were to:

1. Observe your trainer or someone else leading a huddle. Note your observations and prepare to share them with the group. And/ or lead a portion of a huddle under the guidance of your trainer.

■ What did you do well and what could you have done better?

2. Practice active listening among a small group of friends by using each of the "Five Hats" follow-up questions.

■ Who did you meet with? What did you learn from this experience?

3. Study the huddle examples at the back of the book and use them as a guide to create your own huddle session. Bring a copy of your huddle session to your next training to share with your trainer and the others in your training group.

■ Share what you came up with and receive feedback from others in your training session.

Reflect on Your Learning

■ Where did you grow the most in this competency?

■ What next step do you need to take to continue to grow in this competency?

Module 5: Recruiting New Leaders

In this module we will focus on deepening your passion and developing your competency of recruiting new leaders.

 Deepen Your Character: Passion

Let's begin by focusing on the character portion of this study. In this module the focus is on: **Passion**—*Leaders are filled with a fervent drive toward the cause God has given them.*

Read Colossians 1:28–29 together.

Colossians 1:28–29

He is the one we proclaim, admonishing and teaching everyone with all wisdom, so that we may present everyone fully mature in Christ. To this end I strenuously contend with all the energy Christ so powerfully works in me.

■ Who do you know who has a passion for Christ you admire?

■ What do you learn from their example?

■ When you read Paul's words in Colossians 1:28–29, what would you like to emulate from his example?

■ What factors are either fueling or extinguishing your passion for God at this time.

■ If we're honest, there are times when we have more passion for God than others. The best way to grow your passion is to start with an honest assessment of where you are presently. Imagine your passion for intimacy with God as a flame. Which of the following three pictures best illustrates your level of passion for intimacy with God right now?

- Why did you choose that picture?

- Write down one insight this exercise reveals about you.

- What one action step could you take to grow in this area?

Develop Your Competency: *Recruiting Leaders*

Now that we've talked about how we can grow in passion, let's talk through what you learned about the competency: **Recruiting Leaders**—*Expand your team by following a deliberate recruitment process.*

- What was the best volunteer role you've ever had? Why?

Four Essentials for Recruiting Leaders

- Which of the four essentials is your strength?

- Which of the four do you need to grow in the most?

- What was your biggest takeaway from this section?

Relationship Plays an Important Role in Recruiting

Imagine your church and area of ministry just experienced a sudden growth spurt. The pastor announces at a small gathering of leaders that he needs all your help in recruiting new leaders to help with this new growth. It's determined that you need to recruit four new leaders in your area of ministry. They would like to have these new leaders in place within the next two months.

- What challenges do you think you would face recruiting these four new leaders?

- What are some of the things you would do over those two months to recruit in a relational way?

- Getting others to say "yes" to our recruitment request requires a degree of leadership influence. Make a list of reasons people say "yes" and a list of reasons people say "no" to volunteer service opportunities.

Recruiting and Keeping Leaders

- If you've recruited anyone in the past, what was the most critical mistake you made in the recruiting process? What did you learn from it?

- Which of the seven steps listed do you think will be the easiest for you? Why?

- Which of the seven steps do you think will be most challenging for you? Why?
- What actions can you take to improve in your area of biggest challenge?

■ As you think of recruiting people to serve on a team, do you feel more nervous or excited? Why?

■ What action steps do you need to take over the next thirty days to improve your recruiting skills?

Put It Into Practice

Developing a new skill requires practice. Discuss with those you are training what they learned about recruiting leaders from their "Put It Into Practice" assignments.

The assignments were to:

1. Interview a volunteer who serves in the community or at church and ask what made him or her agree to serve in that role.

■ Who did you interview? What did you discover?

2. Observe your trainer asking a potential team member or leader to join a team.

■ What aspects of this module's insights did your trainer do well?

■ What did your trainer do intentionally?

■ What would you do differently?

3. Make a list of names of people you know who could potentially serve on your team.

■ In what role would you recruit them to serve?

■ What traits do they have that make them a good fit for that role?

Reflect on Your Learning

■ Where did you grow the most in this competency?

■ What next step do you need to take to continue to grow in this competency?

Module 6: Navigating Conflict

In this module we will focus on deepening your patience and developing your competency of navigating conflict.

 Deepen Your Character: *Patience*

Let's begin by focusing on the character portion of this study. In this module the focus is on: **Patience**—*Leaders must be gentle when navigating conflict and bear with others' shortcomings with the higher goal of developing their spiritual maturity.*

Read Ephesians 4:2–6 together.

Ephesians 4:2–6

Be completely humble and gentle; be patient, bearing with one another in love. Make every effort to keep the unity of the Spirit through the bond of peace. There is one body and one Spirit, just as you were called to one hope when you were called; one Lord, one faith, one baptism; one God and Father of all, who is over all and through all and in all.

- As you think about demonstrating patience in the midst of navigating conflict, what part of this passage stands out the most to you? Why?

- Think of a time you saw conflict management in a personal, ministry, or business setting handled in an inappropriate or unwise way? How was impatience part of the problem?

- What was the outcome?

- What are the behaviors unique to you that demonstrate your impatience with others? (For example, raising your voice, talking "down" to others, etc.)

- To assess your patience with others, look at the following statements based on Ephesians 4. Think of a recent situation where you tried to navigate conflict among two or more people. Reflect on your attitudes and behavior. Mark each trait red, yellow or green. Red = I am not demonstrating this area. Yellow = I could be more intentional in this area. Green = I am demonstrating this consistently.

I practiced **humility**, listening before I spoke and putting their need to be heard first.

I was **gentle** in the way I spoke, choosing my words and my tone of voice carefully.

I was **patient** when they frustrated me, disagreed with me and/or the mediation process took much longer than anticipated.

I was willing to **bear with** temporary immaturity in order to develop the group spiritually.

- What is one insight this exercise reveals about your character?

- What is one action step you need to take to grow in that area?

Develop Your Competency: *Navigating Conflict*

Now that we've talked about how we can grow in patience, let's talk through what you learned about the competency: **Navigating Conflict**—*Manage conflict in a way that honors God and those involved.*

Different people respond to conflict in different ways. What is your instinctive reaction when you find yourself having to navigate conflict? Why?

Navigating Conflict Among Team Members

- Think back to previous conflicts you've encountered. What seemed to be the root cause of the conflict? (When sharing in your training session, do not reveal names, sensitive information or give information that would disclose who was involved in the conflict.)

- What did you learn about navigating conflict from those experiences?

- Think of a time when a conflict you were either a part of or were aware of ended with true, healthy reconciliation. What factors helped achieve reconciliation?

Understanding Communication Styles

- Which communication styles have you seen evidenced in your current group or team you're leading? How has that diversity of styles affected team culture?

Steps for Positively Navigating Conflict

■ What are some common mistakes leaders make when navigating conflict?

■ Consider a conflict you've experienced in the past. What mistakes did you make? What communication styles did the people involved use? Reflect on and write out how you would navigate that issue more effectively if you were armed with the information you've learned in this module.

■ Which of the six steps for managing conflict have you mastered? List below. How have you demonstrated your mastery of these steps in the past?

■ Which of the six steps are your weakest? List below. Name one positive outcome that would result from your growth in this area.

Put It Into Practice

Developing a new skill requires practice. Discuss with those you are training what they learned about navigating conflict from their "Put It Into Practice" assignment.

The assignment was to:

Ask a close friend or family member to give you honest feedback on how you typically handle conflict. Reference a specific situation if possible. And you were to ask them questions like: "How do you think I normally respond to conflict? In what way do I handle it well?

What could I do better? How do I come across when I am frustrated? What advice would you give me to better handle conflict as a leader?"

- What did you discover from this exercise?

Reflect on Your Learning

- Where did you grow most in this competency?

- What next step do you need to take to continue to grow in this competency?

Module 7: Review Your Progress

The final step of this training is a post-assessment that your trainee can either complete on their own or with you. Please turn to page 173 for more information.

Auxano delivers the process that leads to real church growth.

Where do you need break-thru clarity?

Learn more about our unique set of integrated, break-thru experiences for church teams at auxano.com

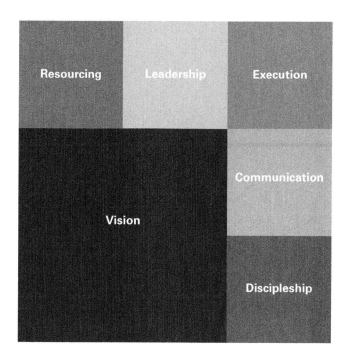

MOVEMENTS
PUBLISHING

100 Movements Publishing is a hybrid publisher, offering the benefits of both traditional and self-publishing.

OUR AUTHORS ARE **RISK-TAKERS,**
PARADIGM-SHIFTERS, INCARNATIONAL
MISSIONARIES, AND **INFLUENTIAL LEADERS**
WHO LOVE THE BODY OF CHRIST AND
WANT TO SPUR HER ON FOR MORE.

Our books aim to inspire and equip disciples
to take hold of their God-given call to make disciples
and to see kingdom impact in every sphere of society.

Changing the Conversation

OUR BOOKS SHIFT PARADIGMS, EQUIP
LEADERS, AND INSPIRE MISSIONAL
DISCIPLES TO PLAY THEIR PART
IN CATALYZING MISSIONAL MOVEMENTS.

For more information, please visit us at 100Mpublishing.com

Printed in Great Britain
by Amazon